MATH

Trailblazers®

A BALANCED MATHEMATICS PROGRAM INTEGRATING SCIENCE AND LANGUAGE ARTS

Unit Resource Guide
Unit 10
Maps and Coordinates

THIRD EDITION

KENDALL/HUNT PUBLISHING COMPANY
4050 Westmark Drive   Dubuque, Iowa 52002

A TIMS® Curriculum
University of Illinois at Chicago

UIC The University of Illinois
at Chicago

The original edition was based on work supported by the National Science Foundation under grant No. MDR 9050226 and the University of Illinois at Chicago. Any opinions, findings, and conclusions or recommendations expressed in this publication are those of the author(s) and do not necessarily reflect the views of the granting agencies.

Printed in the United States of America

1 2 3 4 5 6 7 8 9 10 11 10 09 08 07

Letter Home

Maps and Coordinates

Date: _____

Dear Family Member:

This unit addresses several topics in mathematics. One involves describing the location of objects using numbers. A story about this idea's origin tells how the French philosopher and mathematician René Descartes had a habit of lying in bed until noon every day. One morning he saw a fly crawling on the ceiling in a jagged path and had an inspiration: if he chose one point on the ceiling, he could describe the position of the fly by noting the number of tiles the fly was to the right and in front of this point.

Today mathematicians refer to this system of locating objects as using Cartesian coordinates, in honor of Descartes. This unit will explore Cartesian coordinate grids involving both positive and negative numbers.

Your child will also explore negative numbers in real-life situations, such as temperatures below zero or altitudes below sea level.

Descartes locating a fly

There are many opportunities to assist your child at home with these ideas and other topics in this unit:

- While traveling, locate destinations using coordinates found on the edges of a map.
- Talk about situations when negative numbers appear naturally, such as cold temperatures, altitudes below sea level, or negative checking account balances.

Sincerely,

_____

Carta al hogar

Mapas y coordenadas

Fecha: _____

Estimado miembro de familia:

Esta unidad cubre varios temas relacionados con las matemáticas. Uno de ellos consiste en describir la posición de objetos usando números. Una historia sobre esta idea cuenta cómo el filósofo y matemático francés, René Descartes solía quedarse en la cama hasta el mediodía todos los días. Un día vio una mosca caminando sobre el techo siguiendo un recorrido irregular y tuvo una inspiración: si escogía un punto sobre el techo, podría describir la posición de la mosca contando el número de mosaicos que la mosca estaba hacia la derecha y hacia adelante con respecto a este punto.

Hoy en día los matemáticos llaman a este sistema para localizar objetos "coordenadas cartesianas", en honor a Descartes. En esta unidad, se estudiarán cuadrículas de coordenadas cartesianas que incluyen números positivos y negativos.

Su hijo/a explorará también los números negativos en situaciones de la vida real, tal como temperaturas bajo cero o altitudes bajo el nivel del mar.

Descartes localizando una mosca

Hay muchas oportunidades para asistir a su hijo/a en casa con estas ideas y con otros temas cubiertos en esta unidad:

- Mientras viajan, ubiquen destinos usando las coordenadas que están a los lados de un mapa.
- Hablen sobre situaciones en las que los números negativos aparecen naturalmente, tal como temperaturas frías, altitudes bajo el nivel del mar o saldos negativos de cuentas bancarias.

Atentamente,

_____

Table of Contents

Unit 10
Maps and Coordinates

Outline 2

Background 9

Observational Assessment Record 11

Daily Practice and Problems 13

Lesson 1 *Negative Numbers* 22

Lesson 2 *Introducing Cartesian Coordinates* 36

Lesson 3 *Wherefore Art Thou, Romeo?* 52

Lesson 4 *Mr. Origin* 60

Lesson 5 *Plotting Shapes* 76

Lesson 6 *These Boots Are Made for Sliding* 86

Lesson 7 *These Boots Are Made for Flipping* 100

Lesson 8 *Reading a Map* 115

Lesson 9 *Escher Drawings* 127

Home Practice Answer Key 134

Glossary 137

Unit 10

Outline
Maps and Coordinates

Unit Summary

Estimated Class Sessions **8-14**

This unit starts with a discussion of negative numbers within several real-world contexts, including measuring temperature and tracking money in a bank account. Then, positive and negative numbers are applied to the task of making coordinate maps. The activity *Mr. Origin* extends students' use of coordinates to four quadrants. An Adventure Book *Wherefore Art Thou, Romeo?* emphasizes the importance of the positive and negative signs in coordinate pairs. In optional activities, students develop their spatial visualization skills and their understanding of geometric concepts by investigating the results of flips and slides on shapes in the coordinate plane.

Major Concept Focus

- negative numbers
- four quadrants
- plotting points
- tessellations
- Cartesian coordinates
- coordinate pairs
- reading maps
- Student Rubric: *Knowing*
- slides and flips
- using the scale on a map
- *Adventure Book:* coordinates

Pacing Suggestions

- Students with previous experience with *Math Trailblazers*® worked with coordinates in the first quadrant in third grade. They explored negative numbers in fourth grade. This unit extends their understanding of the coordinate system to four quadrants using negative numbers. If students have not previously worked with these concepts, they will move more slowly through the lessons. Use the maximum number of sessions as a guide for these students. If students have worked with these concepts in previous grades, use the minimum number.

- You can include Lesson 8 *Reading a Map* in a map-reading lesson during social studies time.

Lessons 6, 7, and 9 are optional lessons that provide enrichment and fuller understanding of the Cartesian coordinate system. Use Lessons 6 and 7 if state or local standards call for students to study transformations (flips and slides).

- Lesson 6 *These Boots Are Made for Sliding* shows students how to slide (translate) shapes along one coordinate and then both coordinates.

- Lesson 7 *These Boots Are Made for Flipping* shows students how to flip (reflect) shapes about the horizontal and vertical axes. This lesson includes Assessment Pages *Moving Shapes,* a written assessment for the activities in both Lessons 6 and 7. If you omit either lesson, do not use the assessment.

- Lesson 9 *Escher Drawings* allows students to explore the work of M.C. Escher and use tessellations to create art.

Assessment Indicators

Use the following Assessment Indicators and the *Observational Assessment Record* that follows the Background section in this unit to assess students on key ideas.

A1. Can students represent negative numbers using a number line?

A2. Can students solve problems using negative numbers?

A3. Can students plot points using ordered pairs in the four quadrants?

A4. Can students locate objects or find locations on maps using coordinates?

A5. Can students use a scale map to find distances?

Unit Planner

	Lesson Information	Supplies	Copies/Transparencies

Lesson 1

Negative Numbers

URG Pages 22–35
SG Pages 316–318
DPP A–B
HP Parts 1–2

Estimated Class Sessions

1

Activity
Children expand the number line to include negative numbers. They explore negative numbers in real-world contexts.

Math Facts
DPP item A reviews the multiplication and division facts for the 2s and square numbers.

Homework
1. Assign the Homework section in the *Student Guide*.
2. Assign Parts 1 and 2 of the Home Practice.

Assessment
Use *Questions 8–12* to assess students' progress in solving problems involving negative numbers. Record your observations on the *Observational Assessment Record* or students' *Individual Assessment Record Sheets*.

Supplies:
• indoor/outdoor thermometer, optional

Copies/Transparencies:
• 2 copies of *Two-column Data Table* URG Page 33 per student, optional
• 1 transparency of *Frank's Bank Statement* URG Page 31
• 1 transparency of *Reading a Thermometer* URG Page 32
• 1 copy of *Observational Assessment Record* URG Pages 11–12 to be used throughout this unit
• 1 copy of *Individual Assessment Record Sheet* TIG Assessment section per student, previously copied for use throughout the year

Lesson 2

Introducing Cartesian Coordinates

URG Pages 36–51
SG Pages 319–326
DPP C–F
HP Part 3

Estimated Class Sessions

2-3

Activity
This activity introduces students to the use of Cartesian coordinates for locating objects in a plane. The game *Great Barrier Reef* is introduced.

Math Facts
DPP item E reviews division facts.

Homework
1. Assign *Questions 11–18* in the Explore section.
2. Assign the game as homework.
3. Assign the Homework section in the *Student Guide*.

Assessment
1. Use the Homework section in the *Student Guide* as an assessment.
2. Use Part 3 of the Home Practice as an assessment.

Copies/Transparencies:
• 4 copies plus extras of *Four-Quadrant Grid Paper* URG Page 47 per student or 4 copies plus extras of *Centimeter Grid Paper* URG Page 48 per student with axes drawn
• 1 transparency of *One Quadrant Plus* URG Page 45
• 1 transparency of *Quadrant Overlay* URG Page 46
• 1 transparency of *Four-Quadrant Grid Paper* URG Page 47

Lesson 3

Wherefore Art Thou, Romeo?

URG Pages 52–59
AB Pages 61–76
DPP G–H

Estimated Class Sessions

1

Adventure Book
This book follows the misfortunes of a student who does not understand coordinates and causes chaos in a school play as a result.

Supplies:
• flashlight, optional

	Lesson Information	Supplies	Copies/ Transparencies
Lesson 4 **Mr. Origin** URG Pages 60–75 SG Pages 327–329 DAB Page 165 DPP I–L HP Part 5 *Estimated Class Sessions* **2-3**	**Activity** Students map the location of objects in a room or playground on a four-quadrant coordinate map. They use the map to make predictions about the distance between the objects. **Math Facts** DPP items I and K review the multiplication and division facts for the 2s and the square numbers. **Homework** 1. Have students draw a coordinate map of a room in their home. 2. Students complete the *Label the Axes* Homework Page in the *Discovery Assignment Book.* 3. Assign Part 5 of the Home Practice. **Assessment** Use the *Coordinates: Getting to the Point* Assessment Page to assess students' abilities to graph points.	• 1 meterstick or trundle wheel per student group • 1 Mr. Origin per student group, optional and 1 for the teacher • 7 index cards to label objects • 1 centimeter ruler per student group	• 1 copy of *Coordinates: Getting to the Point* URG Page 71 per student • 2 copies of *Centimeter Grid Paper* URG Page 48 per student • 1 copy of *Three-column Data Table* URG Page 72 per student, optional
Lesson 5 **Plotting Shapes** URG Pages 76–85 SG Pages 330–331 DPP M–N HP Part 4 *Estimated Class Sessions* **1**	**Activity** Children plot ordered pairs in four quadrants, then connect the dots to make shapes. **Homework** 1. Students design their own shape in **Question 5,** which you can assign for homework. 2. Assign Part 4 of the Home Practice. **Assessment** Assess students' abilities to plot points as they complete **Questions 1–3.** Record your observations on the *Observational Assessment Record.*		• several copies of *Four-Quadrant Grid Paper* URG Page 47 per student • several copies of *Half-Centimeter Graph Paper* URG Page 83 per student • 1 transparency of *Four-Quadrant Grid Paper* URG Page 47 • 1 transparency of *Half-Centimeter Graph Paper* URG Page 83, optional
Lesson 6 **These Boots Are Made for Sliding** URG Pages 86–99 SG Pages 332–336 DAB Pages 167–171 *Estimated Class Sessions* **1**	OPTIONAL LESSON— ENRICHMENT MATERIAL **Optional Activity** Children explore slides on a coordinate grid. **Homework** Assign the homework problems in the *Student Guide.*		• several copies of *Four-Quadrant Grid Paper* URG Page 47 per student or several copies of *Centimeter Grid Paper* URG Page 48 per student with axes drawn • 1 copy of *Four-column Data Table* URG Page 94 per student • 1 transparency of *Four-Quadrant Grid Paper* URG Page 47 • 1 transparency of *Slides* DAB Pages 167–171, optional

(Continued)

	Lesson Information	Supplies	Copies/Transparencies
Lesson 7 **These Boots Are Made for Flipping** URG Pages 100–114 SG Pages 337–342 DAB Pages 173–174 *Estimated Class Sessions* **1-2**	OPTIONAL LESSON— ENRICHMENT MATERIAL **Optional Activity** Children explore flipping shapes across the horizontal and vertical axes. **Homework** Assign the Homework section in the *Student Guide.* **Assessment** Use the *Moving Shapes* Assessment Pages as a quiz.	• 1 pair of scissors per student pair	• 1 copy *of Moving Shapes* URG Pages 108–109 per student • several copies of *Four-Quadrant Grid Paper* URG Page 47 per student • 1 copy of *Centimeter Graph Paper* URG Page 110 per student • 1 transparency of *Flips* DAB Pages 173–174, optional • 1 transparency of *Four-Quadrant Grid Paper* URG Page 47
Lesson 8 **Reading a Map** URG Pages 115–126 SG Pages 343–344 DPP O–P HP Part 6 *Estimated Class Sessions* **1**	**Activity** Students practice map-reading skills from the perspective of one and then four quadrants. An assessment using the *Knowing* Student Rubric is included. **Math Facts** DPP item O reviews math facts. **Homework** 1. Assign the Homework section on the *Reading a Map* Activity Pages in the *Student Guide.* 2. Assign Part 6 of the Home Practice. **Assessment** Use the *Carol's Chicago Map* Assessment Pages as an assessment.		• 1 copy of *Carol's Chicago Map* URG Pages 121–122 per student • 1 transparency of *Chicago Grid* URG Page 123 • 1 transparency of *Chicago Map* URG Page 124 • 1 copy of *TIMS Multidimensional Rubric* TIG, Assessment section
Lesson 9 **Escher Drawings** URG Pages 127–133 SG Page 345 *Estimated Class Sessions* **1**	OPTIONAL LESSON— ENRICHMENT MATERIAL **Optional Activity** Children explore the work of M.C. Escher and make their own Escher-like artwork.	• several index cards per student • 1 piece of newsprint or other large paper preferably greater than 8″ × 10″ plus extras • 1 pair of scissors per student • tape	• 1 transparency of *Creating Escher-like Drawings* URG Page 132, optional

Connections

A current list of literature and software connections is available at *www.mathtrailblazers.com*. You can also find information on connections in the *Teacher Implementation Guide* Literature List and Software List sections.

Literature Connections

Suggested Titles

- Knowlton, Jack. *Maps and Globes.* Harper Collins Publishers, New York, 1985.
- Olesky, Walter. *Mapping the World.* Scholastic Press, Inc., New York, 2002.

Software Connections

- *Building Perspective Deluxe* develops spatial reasoning and visual thinking in three dimensions.
- *Make A Map 3D* introduces reading and interpreting maps, direction, distance, and scale on maps.
- *Math Arena* is a collection of math activities that reinforces many math concepts.
- *MicroWorlds EX* is a drawing program that helps students develop spatial reasoning and an understanding of coordinates while making shapes.
- *Mighty Math Number Heroes* poses short answer questions about fractions, number operations, polygons, and probability.
- *National Geographic* on the World Wide Web has many maps and related activities for students.
- *Tessellation Exploration* develops understanding of the geometry of tessellations and allows students to create their own.

Teaching All Math Trailblazers Students

Math Trailblazers lessons are designed for students with a wide range of abilities. The lessons are flexible and do not require significant adaptation for diverse learning styles or academic levels. However, when needed, lessons can be tailored to allow students to engage their abilities to the greatest extent possible while building knowledge and skills.

To assist you in meeting the needs of all students in your classroom, this section contains information about some of the features in the curriculum that allow all students access to mathematics. For additional information, see the Teaching the *Math Trailblazers* Student: Meeting Individual Needs section in the *Teacher Implementation Guide.*

Differentiation Opportunities in this Unit

Games

Use games to promote or extend understanding of math concepts and to practice skills with children who need more practice.

- *Barrier Reef Game* from Lesson 2 *Introducing Cartesian Coordinates*

Journal Prompts

Journal prompts provide opportunities for students to explain and reflect on mathematical problems. They can help both students who need practice explaining their ideas and students who benefit from answering higher order questions. Students with various learning styles can express themselves using pictures, words, and sentences. Teachers can alter journal prompts to suit students' ability levels. The following lessons contain a journal prompt:

- Lesson 6 *These Boots Are Made for Sliding*
- Lesson 7 *These Boots Are Made for Flipping*

DPP Challenges

DPP Challenges are items from the Daily Practice and Problems that usually take more than fifteen minutes to complete. These problems are more thought-provoking and can be used to stretch students' problem-solving skills. The following lessons have DPP Challenges in them:

- DPP Challenge B from Lesson 1 *Negative Numbers*
- DPP Challenge F from Lesson 2 *Introducing Cartesian Coordinates*
- DPP Challenge N from Lesson 5 *Plotting Shapes*
- DPP Challenge P from Lesson 8 *Reading a Map*

Extensions

Use extensions to enrich lessons. Many extensions provide opportunities to further involve or challenge students of all abilities. Take a moment to review the extensions prior to beginning this unit. Some extensions may require additional preparation and planning. The following lessons contain extensions:

- Lesson 1 *Negative Numbers*
- Lesson 3 *Wherefore Art Thou, Romeo?*
- Lesson 4 *Mr. Origin*
- Lesson 5 *Plotting Shapes*
- Lesson 7 *These Boots Are Made for Flipping*
- Lesson 8 *Reading a Map*

Unit 10

Background
Maps and Coordinates

This unit introduces negative numbers within real-world contexts, including measuring temperature and tracking money in a bank account. Then positive and negative numbers are applied to the task of making coordinate maps. Later in this unit, children develop their spatial visualization skills and understanding of geometric concepts by exploring coordinate geometry.

Students locate objects relative to a plastic figure called Mr. Origin. Mr. Origin is based on a figure invented by Robert Karplus, a physicist who became interested in elementary education and spent a year in Geneva studying with the Swiss psychologist Jean Piaget. In our first- and second-grade activities on mapping and coordinates, Mr. Origin was positioned on a line to represent the origin, or reference point. Then students could determine an object's location by its distance and direction from Mr. Origin. In first grade, the distance from Mr. Origin to the object was measured in links, and the direction was given as left or right. In second grade, the distance was measured in centimeters, and the direction was given as left, right, front, or back. In third grade, an object's location was determined by using two numbers, a left/right coordinate and a front/back coordinate. In this fifth-grade unit, Mr. Origin is positioned at the intersection of the horizontal and vertical axes (the x and y axes) so students must give both a left/right and a front/back measurement using positive and negative numbers.

Figure 1: *Mr. Origin*

Describing the location of an object on a flat surface by using two numbers called *coordinates* is an idea dating back to the 17th century. One story of this idea's beginning, which may not be entirely factual, tells how the French philosopher and mathematician René Descartes had a habit of lying in bed until noon every day thinking about his current mathematical or philosophical problem. One morning, he was working on a particularly tough problem—how to describe the position of an object using numbers. As he gazed at the tiled ceiling, he saw a fly crawling in a jagged path. Suddenly, he had a flash of inspiration. If he chose one point, which we now call the *origin*, he could describe the fly's position with respect to this point by using two numbers: the number of tiles the fly was to the right of the origin and the number of tiles the fly was to the front of the origin.

Figure 2: *Descartes describes the fly's location.*

Locating objects in this way is now known as using **Cartesian coordinates** (in honor of Descartes). Descartes' great insight is that we do not need a tile ceiling or floor to locate an object. We just need an origin and perpendicular axes; the "tiles" can be imaginary. Mathematicians generally label the horizontal axis the x-axis and label the vertical axis the y-axis. This terminology is used in this unit.

There are several major ideas in the lessons on coordinates. First, the notion that directions—right, left, back, and front—depend on choosing a reference point, the **origin.** Second, an object's location can be specified by giving two distances with their directions (the **coordinates**). Third, these coordinates can be plotted on graph paper to make a map. Finally, measurements on the map are usually not the same as distances in the real world. But if we use the same scale on both axes, we can use that scale and the map to estimate distances in the real world.

In Lessons 6 and 7, students use coordinates to draw shapes (polygons) on a coordinate grid. They then explore how a change in coordinates affects a shape. For example, if they add 5 to all the x coordinates of the vertices of a shape, then this translates (slides) the shape 5 units to the right. In addition to translations, they explore some reflections (flips). These lessons are optional.

Finally, the notion of slides is used to explore ways to make tessellations, that is, repeating patterns that cover any flat surface without gaps. In a third optional lesson, students explore the work of the famous artist

M.C. Escher. Many of Escher's drawings are based on tessellating shapes. The activity allows children to create their own Escher-like drawings.

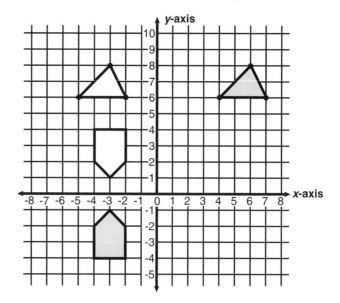

Figure 3: *A slide (9 units to the right) moves one triangle onto the other triangle; a flip (over the x-axis) moves one arrow onto the other arrow.*

Observational Assessment Record

(A1) Can students represent negative numbers using a number line?

(A2) Can students solve problems using negative numbers?

(A3) Can students plot points using ordered pairs in the four quadrants?

(A4) Can students locate objects or find locations on maps using coordinates?

(A5) Can students use a scale map to find distances?

(A6) _____

(A7) _____

Name	A1	A2	A3	A4	A5	A6	A7	Comments
1.								
2.								
3.								
4.								
5.								
6.								
7.								
8.								
9.								
10.								
11.								
12.								
13.								

Name	A1	A2	A3	A4	A5	A6	A7	Comments
14.								
15.								
16.								
17.								
18.								
19.								
20.								
21.								
22.								
23.								
24.								
25.								
26.								
27.								
28.								
29.								
30.								
31.								
32.								

Unit 10

Daily Practice and Problems
Maps and Coordinates

A DPP Menu for Unit 10

Two Daily Practice and Problems (DPP) items are included for each class session listed in the Unit Outline. A scope and sequence chart for the DPP is in the *Teacher Implementation Guide*.

Icons in the Teacher Notes column designate the subject matter of each DPP item. The first item in each class session is always a Bit and the second is either a Task or Challenge. Each item falls into one or more of the categories listed below. A menu of the DPP items for Unit 10 follows.

N Number Sense	✖ Computation	🕐 Time	🔷 Geometry
C, D, F–L, N	B–D, H–L	B	N

$\frac{5}{\times 7}$ Math Facts	$ Money	🎵 Measurement	📏 Data
A, E, I, K, O	B, H	G, N	H, M, N, P

The *Daily Practice and Problems and Home Practice Guide* in the *Teacher Implementation Guide* includes information on how and when to use the DPP.

Review of Math Facts

By the end of fourth grade, students in *Math Trailblazers* are expected to demonstrate fluency with all the facts. The DPP for this unit continues the systematic approach to reviewing the multiplication and division facts. This unit reviews the 2s and square numbers.

For more information about the distribution of the math facts, see the TIMS Tutor: *Math Facts* in the *Teacher Implementation Guide*. Also refer to the *Grade 5 Facts Resource Guide*. For information about fact practice throughout Units 9–16, see the DPP guide for Unit 9.

Daily Practice and Problems

Student Questions	Teacher Notes

A Fact Practice

Solve for *n*.

A. $9 \div n = 3$ B. $16 \div n = 8$

C. $6 \times n = 36$ D. $2 \times n = 12$

E. $n \div 10 = 10$ F. $n \div 8 = 8$

G. $n \times 5 = 25$ H. $n \times 9 = 81$

I. $7 \times 7 = n$ J. $2 \times 9 = n$

TIMS Bit

A. $n = 3$

B. $n = 2$

C. $n = 6$

D. $n = 6$

E. $n = 100$

F. $n = 64$

G. $n = 5$

H. $n = 9$

I. $n = 49$

J. $n = 18$

B Salary

Tim worked the following hours last week.

Monday: 8:30 – 4:30

Tuesday: 8:15 – 5:00

Wednesday: 7:30 – 5:15

Thursday: 8:00 – 4:30

Friday: 7:45 – 4:15

1. How many hours did he work in all?

2. Tim gets paid $8 an hour for the first 40 hours. He gets paid $12 for any overtime. How much did Tim earn last week?

TIMS Challenge

1. $43\frac{1}{2}$ hours or 43.5 hours

2. $40 \times 8 = \$320$;
   3.5 hours $\times$ 12 = $42;
   $362

Student Questions	Teacher Notes

 Division Practice

TIMS Bit

Use a calculator to solve the following division problems. Express the remainder as a whole number. Estimate to be sure your answer is reasonable.

A. 175 R4

B. 3535 R6

C. 67 R365

A. $4204 \div 24 =$

B. $63{,}636 \div 18 =$

C. $27{,}500 \div 405 =$

D **Which Is Greater?**

TIMS Task

Compare each pair of division problems. Copy each pair and fill in the box with $<$, $>$, or $=$. Try to find the answers without dividing. Be prepared to explain your thinking.

Encourage students to explain their reasoning during class discussion.

A. $16 \div 2 \ \boxed{} \ 16 \div 3$

A. $>$

B. $18 \div 4 \ \boxed{} \ 18 \div 3$

B. $<$

C. $48 \div 4 \ \boxed{} \ 48 \div 3$

C. $<$

D. $471 \div 4 \ \boxed{} \ 471 \div 3$

D. $<$

E. $471 \div 4 \ \boxed{} \ 471 \div 7$

E. $>$

F. $1000 \div 8 \ \boxed{} \ 1000 \div 12$

F. $>$

G. $1052 \div 8 \ \boxed{} \ 1176 \div 8$

G. $<$

H. $1057 \div 432 \ \boxed{} \ 100 \div 89$

H. $>$

E Practicing the Facts

A. $20 \div 2 =$

B. $4 \div 2 =$

C. $14 \div 7 =$

D. $100 \div 10 =$

E. $10 \div 5 =$

F. $9 \div 3 =$

G. $6 \div 3 =$

H. $64 \div 8 =$

I. $18 \div 2 =$

TIMS Bit

A. 10   B. 2

C. 2   D. 10

E. 2   F. 3

G. 2   H. 8

I. 9

F What a Squeeze!

Write 5 mixed numbers that are between $1\frac{1}{3}$ and $1\frac{5}{8}$.

TIMS Challenge

Answers might include:

$1\frac{3}{8}$, $1\frac{1}{2}$, $1\frac{6}{11}$, $1\frac{5}{12}$, $1\frac{8}{15}$.

G Wintry Weather

One winter day in Chicago, the low temperature was -6°F. The following day, the low temperature was 16°F. What was the difference in the low temperatures between the two days?

TIMS Bit

22 degrees

Medians and Means

Frank's sister, Mary Lou, is a waitress at a restaurant. She keeps track of the tips she receives daily. Here are the total tips she received last week (Monday through Friday): $53.02, $76.39, $20.16, $58.35, and $125.67.

Terry is interested in working at the same restaurant as Mary Lou. She wants to know if the customers tip well. She asks Mary Lou, "On average, do you bring home more or less than $60 a day in tips?" Based on this week's tips, how should Mary Lou answer this question?

TIMS Task

Answers will vary. The median is $58.35 and the mean is $66.72. Since the mean is over $60, some students may say it is fair for Mary Lou to say she does on average bring home more than $60 a day in tips. Other students might say the median more fairly reflects Mary Lou's data because one day she brought home more than twice $60, which increased the mean. Since on three out of the five days she brought home less than $60, she might tell Terry that she does not bring home, on average, more than $60 a day.

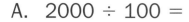 **Dividing by Multiples of Ten**

A. 2000 ÷ 100 =

B. 16,000 ÷ 200 =

C. 40,000 ÷ 2 =

D. 160 ÷ 40 =

E. 25,000 ÷ 50 =

F. 80,000 ÷ 40 =

G. 1400 ÷ 7 =

H. 900 ÷ 3 =

I. 8100 ÷ 900 =

TIMS Bit

A. 20

B. 80

C. 20,000

D. 4

E. 500

F. 2000

G. 200

H. 300

I. 9

J Practice

Solve the following using paper and pencil only. Estimate to make sure each answer is reasonable.

A. $832 \times 12 =$

B. $7850 \div 45 =$

C. $2824 - 1586 =$

D. $178 \times 0.3 =$

E. $4758 + 2517 =$

F. $2804 \div 79 =$

TIMS Task

A. 9984

B. 174 R20

C. 1238

D. 53.4

E. 7275

F. 35 R39

K Multiplying and Dividing by Multiples of Ten

A. $80 \times 800 =$

B. $60 \times 200 =$

C. $90 \times 200 =$

D. $3600 \div 60 =$

E. $4900 \div 70 =$

F. $10,000 \div 50 =$

TIMS Bit

A. 64,000

B. 12,000

C. 18,000

D. 60

E. 70

F. 200

Fractions

1. Use paper and pencil to add or subtract the fractions below. Estimate to be sure your answers are reasonable.

   A. $\frac{3}{8} + \frac{1}{4} =$

   B. $\frac{4}{5} + \frac{2}{3} =$

   C. $\frac{11}{12} - \frac{1}{3} =$

   D. $\frac{8}{9} - \frac{1}{3} =$

   E. $\frac{11}{12} + \frac{1}{6} =$

   F. $\frac{7}{10} - \frac{2}{5} =$

2. Explain your estimation strategy for Question 1E.

TIMS Task

1. A. $\frac{5}{8}$

   B. $\frac{22}{15}$ or $1\frac{7}{15}$

   C. $\frac{7}{12}$

   D. $\frac{5}{9}$

   E. $\frac{13}{12}$ or $1\frac{1}{12}$

   F. $\frac{3}{10}$

2. Strategies will vary. One possible response:

   $\frac{11}{12}$ is close to one and $\frac{1}{6}$ is small, so the answer will be a little more than one.

 What's the Probability?

Roberto rolls a number cube. The six faces show the numbers 1, 2, 3, 4, 5, and 6. What's the probability that he will roll:

A. a number less than 3?

B. an odd number?

TIMS Bit

A. $\frac{2}{6} = \frac{1}{3}$ (the numbers 1 and 2 are possible)

B. $\frac{3}{6} = \frac{1}{2}$ (odd numbers include 1, 3, 5)

Coordinates

Use a piece of graph paper. Scale the horizontal and vertical axes by ones up to 10.

The midpoint of a line segment divides the line into two equal halves. The midpoint O of the line segment $\overline{LM}$ is at (6, 4). The endpoint M has coordinates (10, 5). Plot O and M. What are the coordinates of the endpoint L?

TIMS Challenge

Children can extend the line OM through the midpoint and then use a ruler along the line of the graph to find a distance OL equal to OM. The coordinates of L are (2, 3).

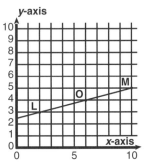

 Practice: 2s and Squares

A. $10 \div 5 =$

B. $25 \div 5 =$

C. $20 \div 2 =$

D. $6 \div 3 =$

E. $4 \div 2 =$

F. $9 \div 3 =$

G. $36 \div 6 =$

H. $8 \div 2 =$

I. $100 \div 10 =$

J. $12 \div 2 =$

K. $64 \div 8 =$

L. $14 \div 7 =$

M. $16 \div 2 =$

N. $49 \div 7 =$

O. $16 \div 4 =$

P. $18 \div 9 =$

Q. $81 \div 9 =$

TIMS Bit

A. 2   B. 5

C. 10   D. 2

E. 2   F. 3

G. 6   H. 4

I. 10   J. 6

K. 8   L. 2

M. 8   N. 7

O. 4   P. 2

Q. 9

Slow and Steady

Four children race their pet turtles. The turtles are named Tee Tee, Truth, Pokey, and Speedy. They used their pets' favorite foods (strawberries, lettuce, cantaloupe, and beets) to get them to cross the finish line. Read these clues to find which food each turtle likes best and in what order they finished the race.

Clues:

A. Truth finished before the turtle who loves lettuce and the turtle who craves cantaloupe, but after Tee Tee.

B. Pokey finished after the turtle who loves strawberries and the turtle with a taste for beets, but before the turtle who prefers cantaloupe.

C. Truth does not like strawberries.

TIMS Challenge

Tee Tee: strawberries, 1st

Truth: beets, 2nd

Pokey: lettuce, 3rd

Speedy: cantaloupe, 4th

Allow students to try solving this problem in pairs or in groups of three. Encourage students to extract all information from each clue before moving to the next clue. Encourage students to share their solution strategies.

After students are given an appropriate amount of time on their own, devising their own solution strategies, you might help them organize their information in a table like the following. As students read each clue, they write "yes" in a box when the information matches a turtle, favorite food, or place. They write "no" if the information rules out a turtle, food, or place.

	strawberries	lettuce	cantaloupe	beets	1st place	2nd place	3rd place	4th place
Tee Tee	Y	N	N	N	Y	N	N	N
Truth	N	N	N	Y	N	Y	N	N
Pokey	N	Y	N	N	N	N	Y	N
Speedy	N	N	Y	N	N	N	N	Y
1st place	Y	N	N	N				
2nd place	N	N	N	Y				
3rd place	N	Y	N	N				
4th place	N	N	Y	N				

Lesson 1

Negative Numbers

Lesson Overview

Estimated Class Sessions

1

Negative numbers are frequently found in our everyday lives. This activity explores the use of negative numbers on thermometers, in bank statements, and in determining altitudes.

Key Content

- Exploring negative numbers.
- Representing negative numbers using a number line.
- Solving problems involving negative numbers.

Key Vocabulary

- negative numbers
- positive numbers

Math Facts

Assign DPP item A, which reviews the multiplication and division facts for the 2s and square numbers.

Homework

1. Assign the Homework section in the *Student Guide*.
2. Assign Parts 1 and 2 of the Home Practice.

Assessment

Use *Questions 8–12* to assess students' progress in solving problems involving negative numbers. Record your observations on the *Observational Assessment Record* or students' *Individual Assessment Record Sheets*.

Curriculum Sequence

Before This Unit

Negative Numbers

In Grade 4 Unit 3 Lesson 6 *What's Below Zero?,* students were introduced to negative numbers. Students explored negative numbers in the context of temperatures, bank balances, and altitudes.

After This Unit

Negative Numbers

Students will continue to explore negative numbers throughout the Daily Practice and Problems and the Home Practice.

Materials List

Supplies and Copies

Student	Teacher
Supplies for Each Student	**Supplies** • indoor/outdoor thermometer, optional
Copies • 2 copies of *Two-column Data Table* per student, optional (*Unit Resource Guide* Page 33)	**Copies/Transparencies** • 1 transparency of *Frank's Bank Statement* (*Unit Resource Guide* Page 31) • 1 transparency of *Reading a Thermometer* (*Unit Resource Guide* Page 32) • 1 copy of *Observational Assessment Record* to be used throughout this unit (*Unit Resource Guide* Pages 11–12)

All blackline masters including assessment, transparency, and DPP masters are also on the Teacher Resource CD.

Student Books
Negative Numbers (*Student Guide* Pages 316–318)

Daily Practice and Problems and Home Practice
DPP items A–B (*Unit Resource Guide* Page 14)
Home Practice Parts 1–2 (*Discovery Assignment Book* Page 161)

Note: Classrooms whose pacing differs significantly from the suggested pacing of the units should use the Math Facts Calendar in Section 4 of the *Facts Resource Guide* to ensure students receive the complete math facts program.

Assessment Tools
Observational Assessment Record (*Unit Resource Guide* Pages 11–12)
Individual Assessment Record Sheet (*Teacher Implementation Guide,* Assessment Section)

Daily Practice and Problems

Suggestions for using the DPPs are on page 29.

A. Bit: Fact Practice (URG p. 14)

Solve for *n*.

A. $9 \div n = 3$ B. $16 \div n = 8$

C. $6 \times n = 36$ D. $2 \times n = 12$

E. $n \div 10 = 10$ F. $n \div 8 = 8$

G. $n \times 5 = 25$ H. $n \times 9 = 81$

I. $7 \times 7 = n$ J. $2 \times 9 = n$

B. Challenge: Salary (URG p. 14)

Tim worked the following hours last week.

Monday: 8:30 – 4:30

Tuesday: 8:15 – 5:00

Wednesday: 7:30 – 5:15

Thursday: 8:00 – 4:30

Friday: 7:45 – 4:15

1. How many hours did he work in all?
2. Tim gets paid $8 an hour for the first 40 hours. He gets paid $12 for any overtime. How much did Tim earn last week?

Use the *Frank's Bank Statement* Transparency Master to pose the following problem to your class:

- *Pretend Frank has a bank account he has forgotten about. There is $25 in it. The bank is now taking $5 from the account every month as a service charge. How many months before his account is empty?* (5 months. His account will be empty in June. Have the class work this out on the transparency.)

- *The bank continues to take $5 out every month. How might this appear on the bank statement?*

  Introduce **negative numbers** to show amounts less than zero. Explain that because Frank's bank balance becomes less than zero, Frank is in debt. He owes money. Have the class show the balance in Frank's account for the next six months.

- *How much money will Frank have in December?* (Frank will have -$30 or be $30 in debt as shown in Figure 4. Explain to students that this is just pretend because most banks will not allow accounts to keep falling month after month.)

Month	Service Charge	Balance
January	-	$25
February	$5	$20
March	$5	$15
April	$5	$10
May	$5	$5
June	$5	$0
July	$5	-$5
August	$5	-$10
September	$5	-$15
October	$5	-$20
November	$5	-$25
December	$5	-$30

Figure 4: *Frank's completed bank statement*

Draw a number line as shown in Figure 5 on the overhead. In the center of the line, put a "0." To the right of the "0" equally space the numbers 1 to 10. To the left, equally space the numbers -1 to -10. Explain that this number line is like those familiar to students, except it has been expanded.

Content Note

Reading the Negative/Minus (-) Sign. The amount "-$5" can be read as "negative $5" or "minus $5." Many teachers choose to read a number below zero as negative, saving the use of the word "minus" to denote subtraction. However, the word "minus" is used regularly in weather forecasts and in other real-world contexts. Children should be aware that both words are used.

Just as **positive numbers** (numbers greater than zero) go on forever, negative numbers do the same in the opposite direction. The arrows at the ends of the line indicate this.

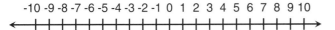

-10 -9 -8 -7 -6 -5 -4 -3 -2 -1 0 1 2 3 4 5 6 7 8 9 10

Figure 5: *Expanding the number line*

Ask students to name other circumstances in which they have heard of negative numbers. Students may think of temperatures. Pose the following problem:

* *The temperature at 9:00 A.M. was -10°F. The temperature at noon is 5°F. What is the change in temperature?*

Encourage students to use the number line to solve this problem. Note that temperatures in this country are most often reported using the Fahrenheit scale, which indicates the boiling point of water at 212°F and freezing at 32°F. Then, ask:

* *The coldest temperature ever recorded in the United States (as of 2002) was -80°F. It was recorded at Prospect Creek Camp, Alaska, on January 23, 1971. The highest temperature was 134°F. It was recorded July 10, 1913 at Death Valley, California. What is the difference between the two temperatures?* (214 degrees. Encourage students to think of a thermometer.)

Altitude is another very common context that requires negative numbers. Pose the following problem:

* *The highest point in California is Mount Whitney, at 14,494 feet. Just 85 miles away is the lowest point, Death Valley, which is 282 feet below sea level. Sea level is considered "zero" feet. We can say that Death Valley is at -282 feet. What is the difference between the two points?* (14,776 feet. Encourage students to use a number line.)

Use the *Negative Numbers* Activity Pages in the *Student Guide* to provide further in-class discussion and homework. This time, the number line takes the form of a thermometer. If you have access to an indoor or outdoor thermometer, show it to the class. If necessary, use the *Reading a Thermometer* Transparency Master to review how to read a thermometer.

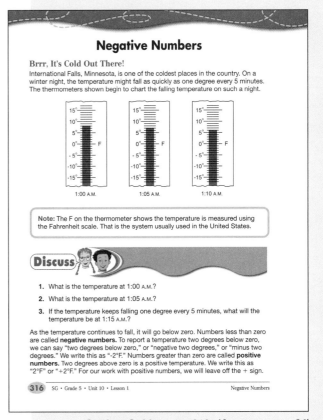

Student Guide - page 316 *(Answers on p. 34)*

Student Guide - page 317 (Answers on p. 34)

The problems in the *Student Guide* ask students to pretend it is winter in International Falls, Minnesota, that it is 1:00 A.M., and the temperature is falling one degree every 5 minutes. In *Questions 1–3,* students read a thermometer and tell the temperature at 1:00 A.M., 1:05 A.M., and 1:10 A.M. Students then explore how positive and negative numbers are represented on a thermometer *(Question 4).* Negative numbers are preceded by a negative sign, while positive numbers are written as just pure numbers.

In *Questions 5–7,* students complete a table showing a 2-hour weather period and then answer questions about their work. Using a *Two-column Data Table,* students show the change in temperature. Ask:

• *What time is it when the temperature in International Falls goes below zero?* (1:40 A.M.)

Questions 8–12 develop an understanding of negative numbers through change in temperature. Student pairs or groups can solve these problems, then share their results with the class. Use the *Observational Assessment Record* or students' *Individual Assessment Record Sheets* to record their understanding as they work on these problems.

Math Facts

DPP item A reviews the multiplication and division facts for the 2s and the square numbers.

Homework and Practice

- Assign DPP item B, which provides a problem involving time and money.
- Assign the Homework section on the *Negative Numbers* Activity Pages in the *Student Guide*.
- Assign Parts 1 and 2 of the Home Practice, which provide practice with division and skip counting with negative numbers.

Answers for Parts 1 and 2 of the Home Practice are in the Answer Key at the end of this lesson and at the end of this unit.

Assessment

Observe students as they complete *Questions 8–12* on the *Negative Numbers* Activity Pages in the *Student Guide*. Record your observations on the *Observational Assessment Record* or students' *Individual Assessment Record Sheets*.

Extension

During the winter, have students look up the hottest and coldest locations in the United States and find the difference in temperatures. If they have access to data for the year, they can find out when the difference is the largest.

Homework

1. Professor Peabody visited International Falls during the winter. He took a plane from California to Minnesota. The temperature in California was 67°F when Professor Peabody left. The temperature in Minnesota was -12°F when he arrived. What is the difference in the temperatures?

2. Professor Peabody was at an altitude of 100 feet below sea level (-100 feet) in California. His altitude in Minnesota was 600 feet above sea level. How much did his altitude change?

3. Professor Peabody recorded the high and the low temperature each day while visiting International Falls. He recorded his data in a table.

	Monday	Tuesday	Wednesday	Thursday	Friday
High	11°F	4°F	1°F	8°F	14°F
Low	-5°F	-23°F	-14°F	-16°F	3°F

A. Find the difference between the high and the low temperature for each of the days.
B. Which day had the greatest change in temperature?
C. What was the highest and the lowest temperature during the week?
D. What was the change in temperature between the highest and the lowest temperature for the week?

4. Professor Peabody had $213.25 in his checking account when he went to Minnesota. He wrote checks for $45.50 for a tour, $122.75 for lodging, and $42.00 for food.
A. How much money did Professor Peabody have left in his account?
B. Professor Peabody wants to buy a souvenir to take home. The souvenir costs $9.00. Can he pay for the souvenir by check? Why or why not? What would his balance be if he wrote a check for $9.00?

5. When Professor Peabody left International Falls the temperature was -17°F. When he arrived in California, the temperature was 73°F. What was the change in temperature?

318   SG • Grade 5 • Unit 10 • Lesson 1   Negative Numbers

***Student Guide - page 318** (Answers on p. 35)*

Name _____ Date _____

Unit 10 Home Practice

PART 1 Division Practice
Solve the following problems using a paper-and-pencil method or mental math. Write your answers with remainders when necessary.

A. 589 ÷ 4 =   B. 6780 ÷ 5 =

C. 1239 ÷ 62 =   D. 42,000 ÷ 70 =

PART 2 Negative Numbers
1. Skip count by 2s backward from 10 to -10. Write the numbers on the number line as you count. Begin this way: 10, 8, 6, . . .

2. Skip count by 3s backward from 12 to -12. Write the numbers as you count.

3. Skip count forward from -20 to 20 by 4s. Write the numbers as you count. Begin this way: -20, -16, -12, ...

4. Use the number line below to show how you can find the answer to this problem: The temperature is -15°F. If the temperature rises 7 degrees, what will the temperature be?

MAPS AND COORDINATES   DAB • Grade 5 • Unit 10 **161**

***Discovery Assignment Book - page 161** (Answers on p. 35)*

Estimated Class Sessions

1

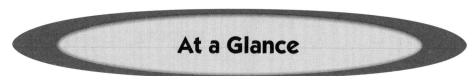

At a Glance

Math Facts and Daily Practice and Problems

Assign DPP items A and B. Bit A reviews the multiplication and division facts for the 2s and square numbers. Challenge B practices problem solving with time and money.

Teaching the Activity

1. Use the *Frank's Bank Statement* Transparency Master to discuss negative numbers in bank accounts.
2. Draw a number line on the board showing both positive and negative numbers.
3. Discuss other contexts such as altitudes in which students may have seen negative numbers.
4. Review reading a thermometer using the *Reading a Thermometer* transparency.
5. Solve the three sample problems in the Lesson Guide involving negative numbers with altitudes and temperatures.
6. Discuss *Questions 1–4* on the *Negative Numbers* Activity Pages in the *Student Guide.*
7. Students complete *Questions 5–12* in pairs or in groups.

Homework

1. Assign the Homework section in the *Student Guide.*
2. Assign Parts 1 and 2 of the Home Practice.

Assessment

Use *Questions 8–12* to assess students' progress in solving problems involving negative numbers. Record your observations on the *Observational Assessment Record* or students' *Individual Assessment Record Sheets.*

Extension

Have students look up the hottest and coldest locations in the United States and find the differences in the temperatures.

Answer Key is on pages 34–35.

Notes:

Frank's Bank Statement

Month	Service Charge	Balance
January	-	$25
February	$5	$20

Reading a Thermometer

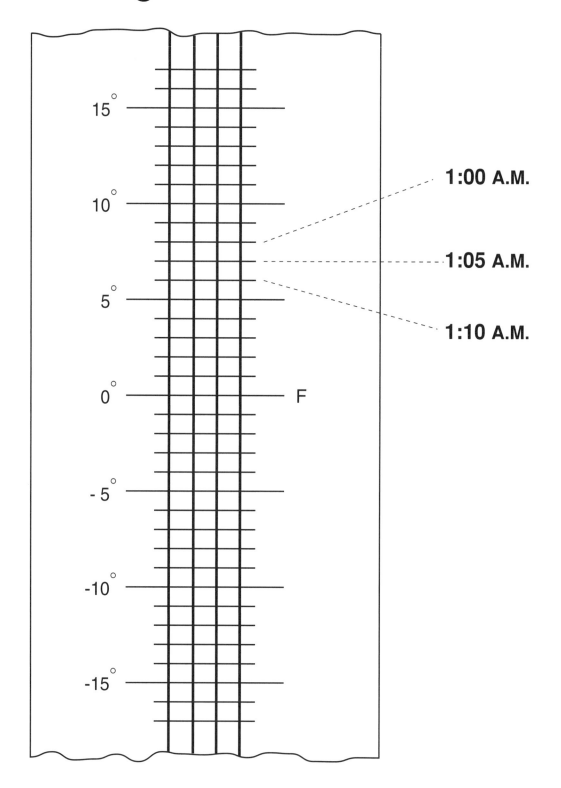

Name _____ Date _____

_____

Two-column Data Table, Blackline Master

Student Guide (pp. 316–317)

Negative Numbers

Negative Numbers

Brrr, It's Cold Out There!
International Falls, Minnesota, is one of the coldest places in the country. On a winter night, the temperature might fall as quickly as one degree every 5 minutes. The thermometers shown begin to chart the falling temperature on such a night.

1:00 A.M.   1:05 A.M.   1:10 A.M.

Note: The F on the thermometer shows the temperature is measured using the Fahrenheit scale. That is the system usually used in the United States.

Discuss

1. What is the temperature at 1:00 A.M.?

2. What is the temperature at 1:05 A.M.?

3. If the temperature keeps falling one degree every 5 minutes, what will the temperature be at 1:15 A.M.?

As the temperature continues to fall, it will go below zero. Numbers less than zero are called **negative numbers**. To report a temperature two degrees below zero, we can say "two degrees below zero," or "negative two degrees," or "minus two degrees." We write this as "-2°F." Numbers greater than zero are called **positive numbers**. Two degrees above zero is a positive temperature. We write this as "2°F" or "+2°F." For our work with positive numbers, we will leave off the + sign.

316 SG • Grade 5 • Unit 10 • Lesson 1   Negative Numbers

Student Guide - page 316

4. Look at the thermometers above Question 1. Which numbers are positive? Which numbers are negative?

5. Make a table like the one below on your own paper. Record the temperature for five minute intervals, beginning at 1:00 A.M. and ending at 3:00 A.M.

International Falls

Time	Temperature
1:00 A.M.	8°F
1:05 A.M.	7°F
1:10 A.M.	6°F
1:15 A.M.	

6. How many degrees did the temperature fall between 1:00 A.M. and 3:00 A.M.?

7. How many degrees did the temperature fall between 1:45 A.M. and 2:15 A.M.?

8. If the temperature keeps falling at the same rate, what will the temperature be at 4:00 A.M.? How do you know?

9. By 10:00 A.M., the temperature had risen to 15°F. How much warmer is the temperature compared to 2:45 A.M.?

10. How much colder is it at 2:30 A.M. than it was at 1:30 A.M.?

11. The dog needed to be let outside at 1:10 A.M. He stayed outside until 1:50 A.M. How much did the temperature fall while the dog was outside?

12. If it is 10°F during the day and it falls to -10°F at night, how many degrees did it fall? (*Hint:* Use the picture of the thermometer.)

Negative Numbers   SG • Grade 5 • Unit 10 • Lesson 1   **317**

Student Guide - page 317

Negative Numbers

1. 8°F

2. 7°F

3. 5°F

4. Negative numbers are preceded by a negative sign.

5.

Time	Temperature
1:00 A.M.	8°F
1:05 A.M.	7°F
1:10 A.M.	6°F
1:15 A.M.	5°F
1:20 A.M.	4°F
1:25 A.M.	3°F
1:30 A.M.	2°F
1:35 A.M.	1°F
1:40 A.M.	0°F
1:45 A.M.	-1°F
1:50 A.M.	-2°F
1:55 A.M.	-3°F
2:00 A.M.	-4°F
2:05 A.M.	-5°F
2:10 A.M.	-6°F
2:15 A.M.	-7°F
2:20 A.M.	-8°F
2:25 A.M.	-9° F
2:30 A.M.	-10°F
2:35 A.M.	-11°F
2:40 A.M.	-12°F
2:45 A.M.	-13°F
2:50 A.M.	-14°F
2:55 A.M.	-15°F
3:00 A.M.	-16°F

6. 24 degrees

7. 6 degrees

8. -28°F. The temperature goes down one degree every five minutes so it goes down 12 degrees every hour. Since it is -16 degrees at 3:00 A.M. it will go down another 12 degrees by 4:00 A.M.

9. 28 degrees

10. 12 degrees colder

11. 8 degrees

12. 20 degrees

Student Guide (p. 318)

Homework

1. 79°F

2. 700 feet

3. **A.** Monday: 16°F

   Tuesday: 27°F

   Wednesday: 15°F

   Thursday: 24°F

   Friday: 11°F

   B. Tuesday

   C. Highest: 14°F; lowest: -23°F

   D. 37 degrees

4. **A.** $3.00

   B. No, he needs $6.00 more; -$6.00

5. 90 degrees

Homework

1. Professor Peabody visited International Falls during the winter. He took a plane from California to Minnesota. The temperature in California was 67°F when Professor Peabody left. The temperature in Minnesota was -12°F when he arrived. What is the difference in the temperatures?

2. Professor Peabody was at an altitude of 100 feet below sea level (-100 feet) in California. His altitude in Minnesota was 600 feet above sea level. How much did his altitude change?

3. Professor Peabody recorded the high and the low temperature each day while visiting International Falls. He recorded his data in a table.

	Monday	Tuesday	Wednesday	Thursday	Friday
High	11°F	4°F	1°F	8°F	14°F
Low	-5°F	-23°F	-14°F	-16°F	3°F

   A. Find the difference between the high and the low temperature for each of the days.

   B. Which day had the greatest change in temperature?

   C. What was the highest and the lowest temperature during the week?

   D. What was the change in temperature between the highest and the lowest temperature for the week?

4. Professor Peabody had $213.25 in his checking account when he went to Minnesota. He wrote checks for $45.50 for a tour, $122.75 for lodging, and $42.00 for food.

   A. How much money did Professor Peabody have left in his account?

   B. Professor Peabody wants to buy a souvenir to take home. The souvenir costs $9.00. Can he pay for the souvenir by check? Why or why not? What would his balance be if he wrote a check for $9.00?

5. When Professor Peabody left International Falls the temperature was -17°F. When he arrived in California, the temperature was 73°F. What was the change in temperature?

318   SG • Grade 5 • Unit 10 • Lesson 1   Negative Numbers

Student Guide - page 318

Discovery Assignment Book (p. 161)

Home Practice*

Part 1. Division Practice

A. 147 R1

B. 1356

C. 19 R61

D. 600

Part 2. Negative Numbers

1. 10, 8, 6, 4, 2, 0, -2, -4, -6, -8, -10

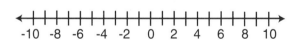

2. 12, 9, 6, 3, 0, -3, -6, -9, -12

3. -20, -16, -12, -8, -4, 0, 4, 8, 12, 16, 20

4. -8°F

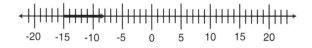

Name _____ Date _____

Unit 10 Home Practice

PART 1 Division Practice

Solve the following problems using a paper-and-pencil method or mental math. Write your answers with remainders when necessary.

   A. 589 ÷ 4 =   **B.** 6780 ÷ 5 =

   C. 1239 ÷ 62 =   **D.** 42,000 ÷ 70 =

PART 2 Negative Numbers

1. Skip count by 2s backward from 10 to -10. Write the numbers on the number line as you count. Begin this way: 10, 8, 6, . . .

2. Skip count by 3s backward from 12 to -12. Write the numbers as you count.

3. Skip count forward from -20 to 20 by 4s. Write the numbers as you count. Begin this way: -20, -16, -12, ...

4. Use the number line below to show how you can find the answer to this problem: The temperature is -15°F. If the temperature rises 7 degrees, what will the temperature be?

MAPS AND COORDINATES   DAB • Grade 5 • Unit 10 **161**

Discovery Assignment Book - page 161

---

*Answers for all the Home Practice in the *Discovery Assignment Book* are at the end of the unit.

Lesson 2

Introducing Cartesian Coordinates

Estimated Class Sessions
2-3

This activity introduces students to the use of Cartesian coordinates using a map of the Great Barrier Reef off the coast of Australia. The first quadrant is introduced and then all four quadrants are explored. Finally, students play a game involving coordinates.

Key Content

- Using coordinates to locate objects, find locations on maps, or plot points on graphs.
- Plotting points using ordered pairs in the four quadrants.

Key Vocabulary

- axes
- Cartesian coordinates
- ordered pair
- origin
- quadrant
- reef

Math Facts

DPP item E reviews division facts.

Homework

1. Assign *Questions 11–18* in the Explore section.
2. Assign the game as homework.
3. Assign the Homework section in the *Student Guide*.

Assessment

1. Use the Homework section in the *Student Guide* as an assessment.
2. Use Part 3 of the Home Practice as an assessment.

Curriculum Sequence

Coordinates

Students have worked with coordinates since first grade. In Unit 8 of third grade, students were introduced to the first quadrant.

Materials List

Supplies and Copies

Student	Teacher
Supplies for Each Student	**Supplies**
Copies	**Copies/Transparencies**
• 4 copies plus extras of *Four-Quadrant Grid Paper* per student (*Unit Resource Guide* Page 47) or 4 copies plus extras of *Centimeter Grid Paper* per student with axes drawn (*Unit Resource Guide* Page 48)	• 1 transparency of *One Quadrant Plus* (*Unit Resource Guide* Page 45) • 1 transparency of *Quadrant Overlay* (*Unit Resource Guide* Page 46) • 1 transparency of *Four-Quadrant Grid Paper* (*Unit Resource Guide* Page 47)

All blackline masters including assessment, transparency, and DPP masters are also on the Teacher Resource CD.

Student Books
Introducing Cartesian Coordinates (*Student Guide* Pages 319–326)

Daily Practice and Problems and Home Practice
DPP items C–F (*Unit Resource Guide* Pages 15–16)
Home Practice Part 3 (*Discovery Assignment Book* Page 162)

Note: Classrooms whose pacing differs significantly from the suggested pacing of the units should use the Math Facts Calendar in Section 4 of the *Facts Resource Guide* to ensure students receive the complete math facts program.

Daily Practice and Problems

Suggestions for using the DPPs are on page 42.

C. Bit: Division Practice (URG p. 15)

Use a calculator to solve the following division problems. Express the remainder as a whole number. Estimate to be sure your answer is reasonable.

A. $4204 \div 24 =$

B. $63,636 \div 18 =$

C. $27,500 \div 405 =$

E. Bit: Practicing the Facts (URG p. 16)

A. $20 \div 2 =$ B. $4 \div 2 =$

C. $14 \div 7 =$ D. $100 \div 10 =$

E. $10 \div 5 =$ F. $9 \div 3 =$

G. $6 \div 3 =$ H. $64 \div 8 =$

I. $18 \div 2 =$

D. Task: Which Is Greater?
(URG p. 15)

Compare each pair of division problems. Copy each pair and fill in the box with <, >, or =. Try to find the answers without dividing. Be prepared to explain your thinking.

A. $16 \div 2$ ☐ $16 \div 3$

B. $18 \div 4$ ☐ $18 \div 3$

C. $48 \div 4$ ☐ $48 \div 3$

D. $471 \div 4$ ☐ $471 \div 3$

E. $471 \div 4$ ☐ $471 \div 7$

F. $1000 \div 8$ ☐ $1000 \div 12$

G. $1052 \div 8$ ☐ $1176 \div 8$

H. $1057 \div 432$ ☐ $100 \div 89$

F. Challenge: What a Squeeze!
(URG p. 16)

Write 5 mixed numbers that are between $1\frac{1}{3}$ and $1\frac{5}{8}$.

Part 1 The Great Barrier Reef

Read The Great Barrier Reef section of the *Introducing Cartesian Coordinates* Activity Pages in the *Student Guide*. This short section sets up the context for work with the coordinate system. You can use a map or globe to remind your students of Australia's location.

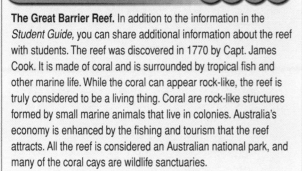

Content Note

The Great Barrier Reef. In addition to the information in the *Student Guide*, you can share additional information about the reef with students. The reef was discovered in 1770 by Capt. James Cook. It is made of coral and is surrounded by tropical fish and other marine life. While the coral can appear rock-like, the reef is truly considered to be a living thing. Coral are rock-like structures formed by small marine animals that live in colonies. Australia's economy is enhanced by the fishing and tourism that the reef attracts. All the reef is considered an Australian national park, and many of the coral cays are wildlife sanctuaries.

Part 2 Exploring the Great Barrier Reef

Read the beginning of the Exploring the Great Barrier Reef Using Cartesian Coordinates section in the *Student Guide*. When looking at the coordinate axes, it is important for students to view the axes as number lines on which they can move back and forth. They need also note that the axes are identified as the x-axis and y-axis. The **axes** are two perpendicular lines that meet at a reference point called the **origin** at location (0, 0). Explain to students that the plural of axis is axes.

Questions 1–10 in the *Student Guide* help students understand the process of locating places on the map using **ordered pairs.** The convention for recording ordered pairs is that the "x" coordinate is shown first, followed by the "y" coordinate. For example, (3, 2) means a location 3 spaces to the right of the origin and 2 spaces up. In earlier grades, children referred to directions right/left and front/back of the origin. Since the example involves a map, it is also appropriate to talk about 3 units east and 2 units north. *Questions 5–10* ask students to locate points with positive x- and y-coordinates.

Introducing Cartesian Coordinates

The Great Barrier Reef

The Great Barrier Reef stretches along the eastern coast of Australia for 1240 miles. A **reef** is a ridge of rocks, sand, or coral in an ocean. Sometimes the reef is covered by water, and sometimes the top of the reef is above the surface and forms islands. The Great Barrier Reef covers an area about half the size of Texas. It is considered the world's largest living structure. For many thousands of years, 400 kinds of reef-building corals have added to the size of the reef. It is home to fish, worms, sea urchins, sea cucumbers, clams, snails, and many other animals.

The Great Barrier Reef is not a solid wall. It is comprised of more than 2600 separate reefs and over 300 islands. Scientists from around the world come to Australia to study the Great Barrier Reef and the animals that make the reef their home. The people of Australia are very proud of their reef and take great care to protect it.

Exploring the Great Barrier Reef Using Cartesian Coordinates

The map on the next page shows one section of the reef. It is covered by a grid system known as **Cartesian coordinates.** This method of mapping was invented by the French philosopher and mathematician René Descartes in the 17th century. It is a very effective method of mapping. To identify the location of an object on a flat surface, we need a reference point, called the **origin**, and two straight lines that pass through the origin at right angles to each other. The lines are called the **axes.** The axes divide the surface into 4 parts called **quadrants.**

Introducing Cartesian Coordinates   SG • Grade 5 • Unit 10 • Lesson 2   **319**

Student Guide - page 319

The map below shows one quadrant of the Cartesian coordinate system placed on top of a map.

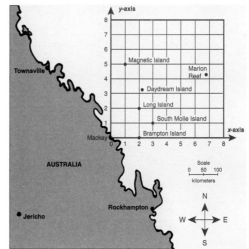

Notice that the axes are named using letters of the alphabet.

1. What name is given to the horizontal axis?
2. What name is given to the vertical axis?

320   SG • Grade 5 • Unit 10 • Lesson 2   Introducing Cartesian Coordinates

Student Guide - page 320 (Answers on p. 49)

The letters *x* and *y* are used the world over to identify the axes of the Cartesian coordinates. On this map, the *x*-axis corresponds to east/west and the *y*-axis to north/south.

3. What is the point of **origin** on the map? In other words, what are the coordinates of the point where the horizontal and vertical axes meet?

4. What do the arrows at the end of the lines mean?

(1, 5) is an example of a location using the Cartesian coordinate system. The 1 tells you to move 1 space to the right (east). The 5 then tells you to move up 5 spaces (north).

5. What island is at location (1, 5) on the map?

Coordinates are always given by saying the *x*-coordinate first, then the *y*-coordinate. For the point (1, 5), the 1 is the *x*-coordinate and the 5 is the *y*-coordinate. (1, 5) is also called an **ordered pair**.

6. What are the coordinates for Long Island?

7. What is located near (2, 3)?

8. What is located at (0, 0)?

9. What are the coordinates for Brampton Island?

10. What is located near (7, 4)?

Find Mackay on the map. Mackay is a city on the eastern coast of Australia. Rockhampton is another city on the coast of Australia. How would you describe Rockhampton's location to someone?

We can expand our coordinate system to include Rockhampton by extending the *x*- and *y*-axes in both directions from (0, 0). By using negative as well as positive numbers, any point can be named in relation to the origin.

The first coordinate of an ordered pair tells us how much to move horizontally (right or left) starting at the origin. The second coordinate tells us how to move vertically (up or down).

Student Guide - page 321   (Answers on p. 49)

Explore

Some examples of ordered pairs and their locations are given here.

The ♥ is at (2, 3).

The ☆ is at (4, -2).

Point A is at (-3, 5).

Point B is at (-2, -5).

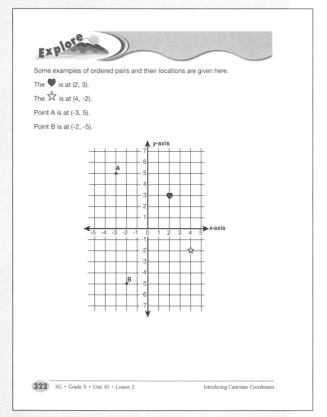

Student Guide - page 322

TIMS Tip

If your classroom has a tiled ceiling, begin this lesson by telling the story of René Descartes. (See the Background or the *Student Guide* for this story's origin.) Place stickers on your ceiling marking the locations of the fly. Then, have students look at the ceiling. Turn off the classroom lights. Shine a flashlight or a laser pointer at the ceiling and describe how René Descartes developed the foundation for the **Cartesian Coordinate System** while lying in bed one day watching a fly move about his ceiling. Have students describe the location of your "fly" on the ceiling using the ceiling tiles as a guide. You can then use the flashlight to move the "fly" to another location for students to describe.

Use the following prompts to introduce all four quadrants:

- *Describe the location of Mackay and Rockhampton, two cities on the eastern coast of Australia.* (Mackay is located at the origin (0, 0) of the map. Rockhampton, however, lies outside the coordinate system of the map. One way to describe its location is in relation to Mackay, that is, about 3 units east and 4 or 5 units south of Mackay.)

Locating Rockhampton can be done more precisely by using the *One Quadrant Plus* Transparency Master to prompt the discussion. Place the *Quadrant Overlay* Transparency over the map to show how to expand the coordinate grid system. Discuss how the grid is divided into four sections (called **quadrants**) by the axes. Show how to use positive and negative numbers to describe any location on the map. Ask:

- *Find the coordinates for Rockhampton, Jericho, and Townsville.* (The coordinates of Rockhampton are approximately (3, -5). The coordinates of Jericho are approximately (-7, -5). The coordinates (-5, 5) locate Townsville.)

Content Note

Maps and Coordinates. Since the Earth is not flat, it is not possible to map large portions of the planet using Cartesian coordinates. For example, longitude lines are not really parallel; they meet at the north and south poles. However, as long as we look at a sufficiently small region, the Earth appears to be flat and Cartesian coordinates can be reasonably accurate.

Mark points in all four quadrants and have students identify the ordered pairs. Repeat until you are comfortable that students understand the structure of the coordinate system. For example, have student volunteers mark the following points on the transparency or draw on the board (-1, 3), (1, 3), (-1, -3), (1, -3). Use *Questions 11–18* for practice. Do these in class or assign as homework.

Part 3 — The *Barrier Reef Game*

The *Barrier Reef Game* gives students a chance to gain experience with the use of Cartesian coordinates. Use a transparency of *Four-Quadrant Grid Paper* to aid the introduction. Students "hide" a pod of whales, a shipwreck, migrating turtles, and a flock of birds on a sheet of *Four-Quadrant Grid Paper*. Have students number the axes.

The game asks children to locate objects "hidden" on the map by their opponent. Objects are located by naming coordinates. A pod of whales uses 5 coordinate points in a row while a shipwreck uses 4 coordinate points in a row, the migrating turtles are 3 coordinate points in a row, and a flock of birds are 2 coordinate points in a row.

If a correct coordinate is given, it must be identified as a "sighting" and the type of object must be identified. Students are asked to use a table to record their attempts, as well as recording them on their game mat. Say, for example, that the game board shown in the *Student Guide* belongs to Player 1. If Player 2 guesses (-1, 0), then Player 1 must say "sighting, a pod of whales." Player 2 should record the coordinates in the data table and write "whales" in the sighting column.

TIMS Tip

Encourage students to place their objects in locations that have negative coordinates. Remind students that the first number in an ordered pair is always the *x*-coordinate.

The game is played by two opponents and a moderator. Have students help you demonstrate the game. Each opponent "hides" the four items by drawing the shapes in pencil on his or her game board. Shapes can only be placed horizontally or vertically. The first player then names an ordered pair and records it in the data table. The opponent says whether or not a sighting has been made. The first player writes "s" for a sighting or "m" for a miss at the point corresponding to the ordered pair. (Alternatively, the player can use markers of two colors and use one color to show hits and the other

---

Name the point at the given coordinates on the following grid.

11. (4, 1)
12. (-2, 0)
13. (-3, -4)
14. (0, -2)

Give the coordinates of the following points.

15. E
16. B
17. C
18. H

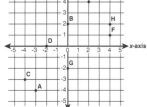

The *Barrier Reef* Game

Players
This is a game for 2 players and a moderator.

Materials
- a sheet of *Four-Quadrant Grid Paper*
- paper for making table

Rules
On a sheet of *Four-Quadrant Grid Paper*, each player "hides" a pod of whales, a shipwreck, migrating turtles, and a flock of birds. An example of the ways to place them on a grid is shown on the following page. Each can be placed either horizontally or vertically.

Introducing Cartesian Coordinates   SG • Grade 5 • Unit 10 • Lesson 2   **323**

Student Guide - page 323 (Answers on p. 50)

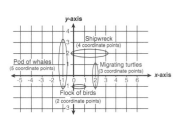

Player 1's Board

Players can use folders to shield their game mats from their opponent. The moderator sits at the players' sides. Each player makes a table like the one shown below on which to record their guesses and sightings. Guesses are also recorded on the game mat itself. On the grid, mark down S for "sighting" and M for "miss."

Player 2's Data Table

X	Y	Sighting?
-1	0	whales
-1	1	whales
-1	-1	whales
-1	2	whales
-1	3	whales
4	-1	miss

The first player begins by naming an ordered pair and recording it in his or her data table. The second player says either "sighting" and the type of object that has been sighted (if there is an object at those coordinates) or "miss" (if there is no object). For example, say the game board shown here belongs to Player 1. If Player 2 guesses (-1, 0), then Player 1 must say "sighting, a pod of whales." Player 2 should record the coordinates in the table and write "whales" in the sighting column. If the first player records a sighting, his or her turn continues. If not, it becomes the second player's turn. The moderator keeps the game fair. The first player to correctly identify all of the coordinates of all of the opponent's objects wins the game.

324   SG • Grade 5 • Unit 10 • Lesson 2   Introducing Cartesian Coordinates

Student Guide - page 324

Historical Note—The Invention of Coordinates

The notion of using coordinates to locate objects was invented by the French philosopher and mathematician, René Descartes. Here is a story that has been told about how he got that idea. Historians are not sure that this story is true, but parts of it are.

Descartes was in the habit of lying in bed in the morning and thinking.

He was working on a problem about how to say where an object is located. The ceiling of his room was covered with square tiles, and a fly was walking around on the ceiling.

He suddenly realized that he could say where the fly was at any time by choosing an origin, and telling how many ceiling tiles the fly was to the right or left and above or below the origin.

Introducing Cartesian Coordinates | SG • Grade 5 • Unit 10 • Lesson 2 | **325**

Student Guide - page 325

to show misses.) If a sighting occurs, the first player goes again. Otherwise the second player begins. The moderator observes the game to keep it fair. The first player to correctly identify all the coordinates of all the opponent's objects wins the game. The moderator then plays the winner, and the loser becomes the moderator.

Math Facts

DPP item E reviews the division facts for the 2s and the square numbers.

Homework and Practice

- Assign DPP items C–F. Items C, D, and E involve division fact practice, remainders, and comparing quotients. Challenge F involves ordering mixed numbers.

- Assign *Questions 11–18* in the Explore section for homework.

- Assign the Homework section in the *Student Guide.*

- Ask students to play the *Barrier Reef Game* at home.

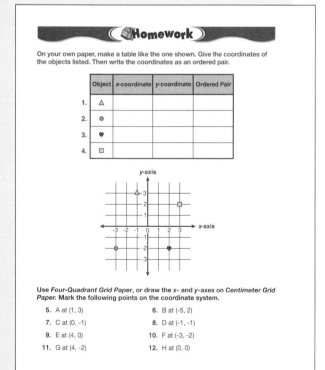

Homework

On your own paper, make a table like the one shown. Give the coordinates of the objects listed. Then write the coordinates as an ordered pair.

	Object	x-coordinate	y-coordinate	Ordered Pair
1.	△			
2.	◎			
3.	♥			
4.	□			

Use *Four-Quadrant Grid Paper,* or draw the x- and y-axes on *Centimeter Grid Paper.* Mark the following points on the coordinate system.

5. A at (1, 3)
6. B at (-5, 2)
7. C at (0, -1)
8. D at (-1, -1)
9. E at (4, 0)
10. F at (-3, -2)
11. G at (4, -2)
12. H at (0, 0)

326 SG • Grade 5 • Unit 10 • Lesson 2   Introducing Cartesian Coordinates

Student Guide - page 326 *(Answers on p. 50)*

- Use the Homework section in the *Student Guide* to assess whether students can identify and plot ordered pairs on a coordinate grid.

- Use Part 3 of the Home Practice to assess students' skills with coordinates.

Answers for Part 3 of the Home Practice are in the Answer Key at the end of this lesson and at the end of this unit.

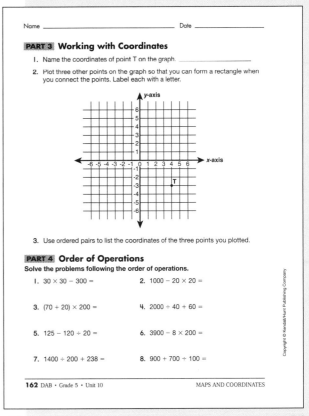

Name _____ Date _____

PART 3 Working with Coordinates

1. Name the coordinates of point T on the graph. _____

2. Plot three other points on the graph so that you can form a rectangle when you connect the points. Label each with a letter.

3. Use ordered pairs to list the coordinates of the three points you plotted.

PART 4 Order of Operations

Solve the problems following the order of operations.

1. $30 \times 30 - 300 =$

2. $1000 - 20 \times 20 =$

3. $(70 + 20) \times 200 =$

4. $2000 \div 40 + 60 =$

5. $125 - 120 \div 20 =$

6. $3900 - 8 \times 200 =$

7. $1400 \div 200 + 238 =$

8. $900 + 700 \div 100 =$

162 DAB · Grade 5 · Unit 10   MAPS AND COORDINATES

Discovery Assignment Book - page 162 *(Answers on p. 51)*

At a Glance

Math Facts and Daily Practice and Problems

DPP item E reviews division facts, and items C and D review division. Challenge F extends fraction number sense.

Part 1. The Great Barrier Reef

Introduce the Great Barrier Reef as a context for the coordinate work.

Part 2. Exploring the Great Barrier Reef

1. Use *Questions 1–10* in the *Student Guide* to introduce work with one quadrant.
2. Use the *One Quadrant Plus* and *Quadrant Overlay* Transparency Masters to extend the work to four quadrants.
3. *Questions 11–18* in the Explore section provide practice naming and finding coordinates.

Part 3. The *Barrier Reef Game*

1. Introduce the game by using a transparency of a game board drawn on *Four-Quadrant Grid Paper.*
2. Allow time for each student to play the game at least once.

Homework

1. Assign *Questions 11–18* in the Explore section.
2. Assign the game as homework.
3. Assign the Homework section in the *Student Guide.*

Assessment

1. Use the Homework section in the *Student Guide* as an assessment.
2. Use Part 3 of the Home Practice as an assessment.

Answer Key is on pages 49–51.

Notes:

One Quadrant Plus

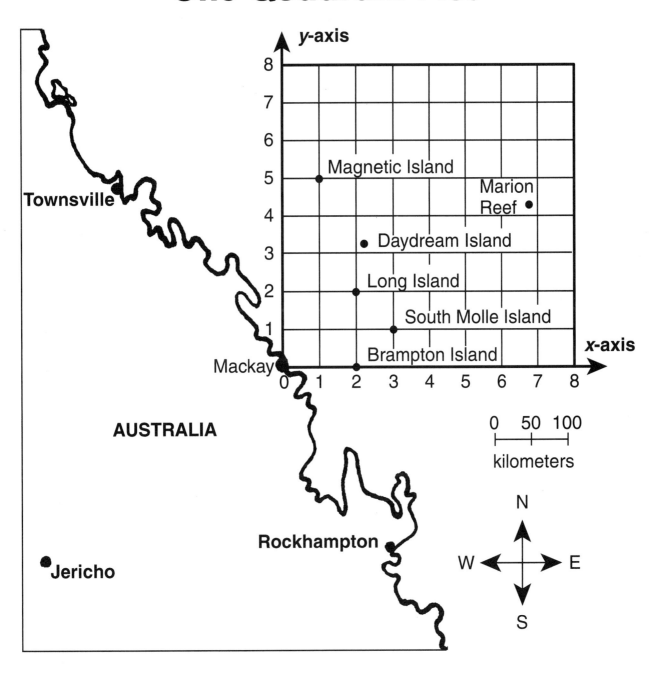

Quadrant Overlay

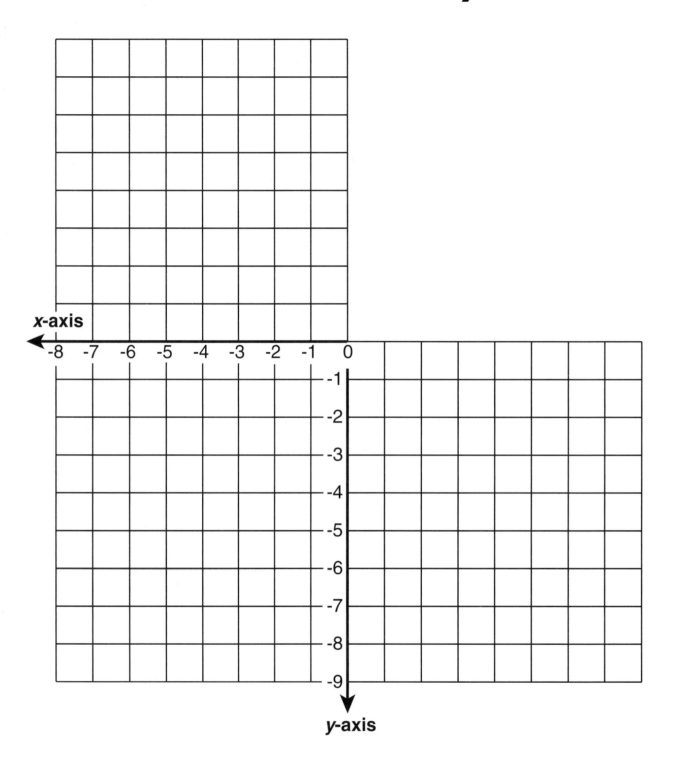

Name _____ Date _____

Four-Quadrant Grid Paper

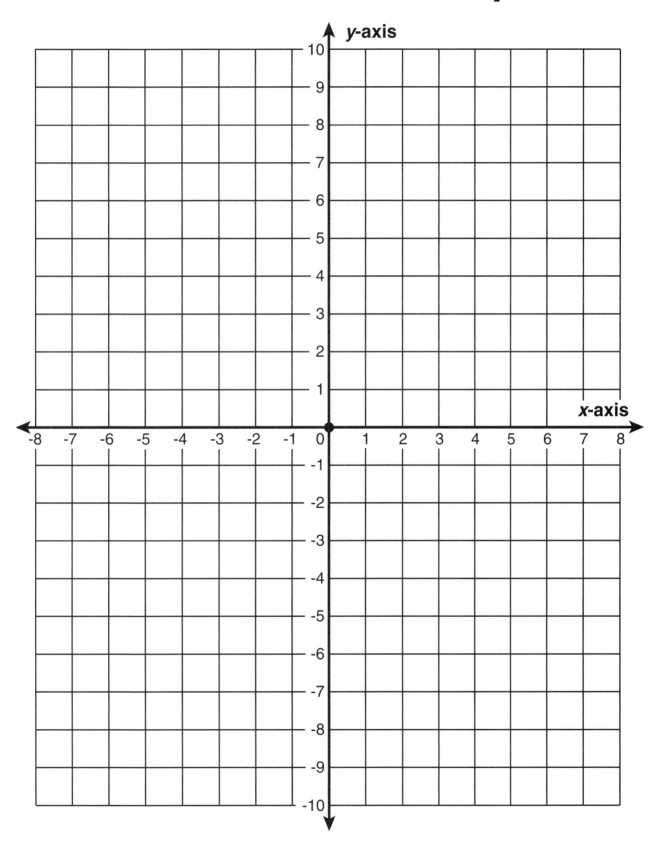

Name _____   Date _____

Centimeter Grid Paper

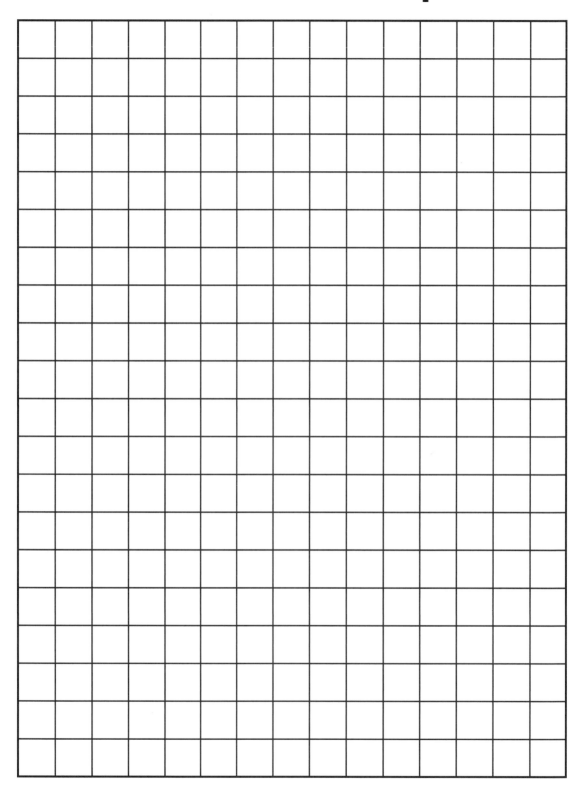

Blackline Master

Student Guide (p. 320)

1. *x*-axis

2. *y*-axis

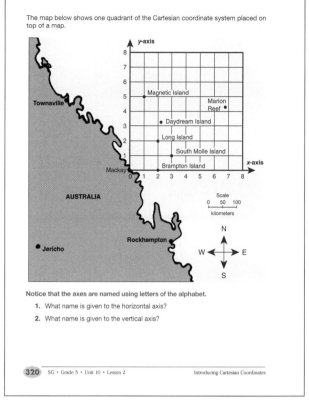

The map below shows one quadrant of the Cartesian coordinate system placed on top of a map.

Notice that the axes are named using letters of the alphabet.

1. What name is given to the horizontal axis?

2. What name is given to the vertical axis?

320   SG • Grade 5 • Unit 10 • Lesson 2   Introducing Cartesian Coordinates

Student Guide - page 320

Student Guide (p. 321)

3. (0, 0)

4. The arrows mean that the lines extend forever.

5. Magnetic Island

6. (2, 2)

7. Daydream Island

8. Mackay

9. (2, 0)

10. Marion Reef

The letters *x* and *y* are used the world over to identify the axes of the Cartesian coordinates. On this map, the *x*-axis corresponds to east/west and the *y*-axis to north/south.

3. What is the point of **origin** on the map? In other words, what are the coordinates of the point where the horizontal and vertical axes meet?

4. What do the arrows at the end of the lines mean?

(1, 5) is an example of a location using the Cartesian coordinate system. The 1 tells you to move 1 space to the right (east). The 5 then tells you to move up 5 spaces (north).

5. What island is at location (1, 5) on the map?

Coordinates are always given by saying the *x*-coordinate first, then the *y*-coordinate. For the point (1, 5), the 1 is the *x*-coordinate and the 5 is the *y*-coordinate. (1, 5) is also called an **ordered pair.**

6. What are the coordinates for Long Island?

7. What is located near (2, 3)?

8. What is located at (0, 0)?

9. What are the coordinates for Brampton Island?

10. What is located near (7, 4)?

Find Mackay on the map. Mackay is a city on the eastern coast of Australia. Rockhampton is another city on the coast of Australia. How would you describe Rockhampton's location to someone?

We can expand our coordinate system to include Rockhampton by extending the *x*- and *y*-axes in both directions from (0, 0). By using negative as well as positive numbers, any point can be named in relation to the origin.

The first coordinate of an ordered pair tells us how much to move horizontally (right or left) starting at the origin. The second coordinate tells us how to move vertically (up or down).

Introducing Cartesian Coordinates   SG • Grade 5 • Unit 10 • Lesson 2   321

Student Guide - page 321

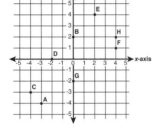

Name the point at the given coordinates on the following grid.

11. (4, 1)

12. (-2, 0)

13. (-3, -4)

14. (0, -2)

Give the coordinates of the following points.

15. E

16. B

17. C

18. H

The *Barrier Reef* Game

Players

This is a game for 2 players and a moderator.

Materials

- a sheet of *Four-Quadrant Grid Paper*
- paper for making table

Rules

On a sheet of *Four-Quadrant Grid Paper*, each player "hides" a pod of whales, a shipwreck, migrating turtles, and a flock of birds. An example of the ways to place them on a grid is shown on the following page. Each can be placed either horizontally or vertically.

Introducing Cartesian Coordinates   SG • Grade 5 • Unit 10 • Lesson 2   **323**

Student Guide - page 323

Student Guide (p. 323)

11. F

12. D

13. A

14. G

15. (2, 4)

16. (0, 2)

17. (-4, -3)

18. (4, 2)

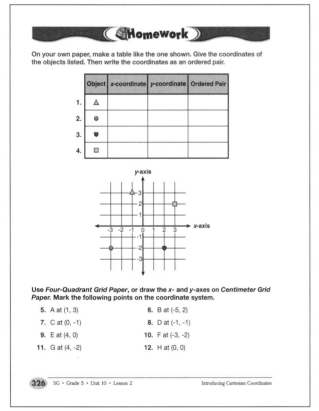

Homework

On your own paper, make a table like the one shown. Give the coordinates of the objects listed. Then write the coordinates as an ordered pair.

Object	x-coordinate	y-coordinate	Ordered Pair
1. △			
2. ◉			
3. ♥			
4. ▢			

Use *Four-Quadrant Grid Paper*, or draw the x- and y-axes on *Centimeter Grid Paper*. Mark the following points on the coordinate system.

5. A at (1, 3)   **6.** B at (-5, 2)

7. C at (0, -1)   **8.** D at (-1, -1)

9. E at (4, 0)   **10.** F at (-3, -2)

11. G at (4, -2)   **12.** H at (0, 0)

326 SG • Grade 5 • Unit 10 • Lesson 2   Introducing Cartesian Coordinates

Student Guide - page 326

Student Guide (p. 326)

Homework

1.–4.

Object	x-coordinate	y-coordinate	Ordered Pair
1. ▲	-1	3	(-1, 3)
2. ●	-3	-2	(-3, -2)
3. ♥	2	-2	(2, -2)
4. ■	3	2	(3, 2)

5.–12.

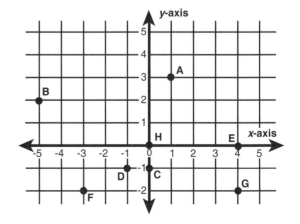

Discovery Assignment Book (p. 162)

Home Practice*

Part 3. Working with Coordinates

1. (4, -3)

2. Answers will vary. A sample rectangle is shown below.

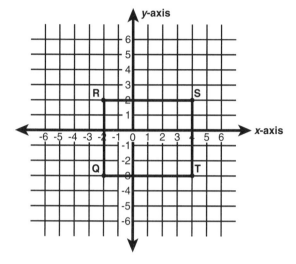

3. Answers will vary. The coordinates of the vertices of the sample rectangle shown in *Question 2* are: Q is at (-2, -3), R is at (-2, 2), and S is at (4, 2).

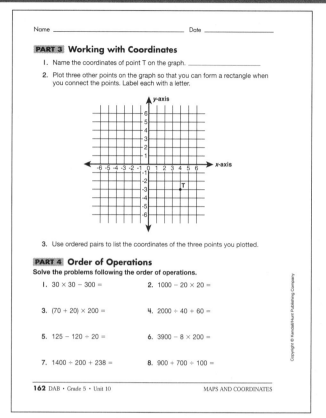

Name _____ Date _____

PART 3 **Working with Coordinates**

1. Name the coordinates of point T on the graph. _____

2. Plot three other points on the graph so that you can form a rectangle when you connect the points. Label each with a letter.

3. Use ordered pairs to list the coordinates of the three points you plotted.

PART 4 **Order of Operations**
Solve the problems following the order of operations.

1. $30 \times 30 - 300 =$
2. $1000 - 20 \times 20 =$
3. $(70 + 20) \times 200 =$
4. $2000 \div 40 + 60 =$
5. $125 - 120 \div 20 =$
6. $3900 - 8 \times 200 =$
7. $1400 \div 200 + 238 =$
8. $900 + 700 \div 100 =$

162 DAB • Grade 5 • Unit 10   MAPS AND COORDINATES

Discovery Assignment Book **- page 162**

*Answers for all the Home Practice in the *Discovery Assignment Book* are at the end of the unit.

Lesson 3

Wherefore Art Thou, Romeo?

Lesson Overview

Estimated Class Sessions

1

In this *Adventure Book,* the stage manager of a troupe of visiting actors recruits a student to use ordered pairs and a computer to control the spotlight for his performers. The student does not understand how ordered pairs work. His lack of understanding of the Cartesian coordinate system wreaks havoc with a production of scenes from *Hamlet* and *Romeo and Juliet.*

Key Content

- Using coordinates.
- Using negative numbers.

Materials List

Supplies and Copies

Student	Teacher
Supplies for Each Student	**Supplies** • flashlight, optional
Copies	**Copies/Transparencies**

All blackline masters including assessment, transparency, and DPP masters are also on the Teacher Resource CD.

Student Books

Wherefore Art Thou, Romeo? (*Adventure Book* Pages 61–76)

Daily Practice and Problems and Home Practice

DPP items G–H (*Unit Resource Guide* Pages 16–17)

Note: Classrooms whose pacing differs significantly from the suggested pacing of the units should use the Math Facts Calendar in Section 4 of the *Facts Resource Guide* to ensure students receive the complete math facts program.

Suggestions for using the DPPs are on page 59.

G. Bit: Wintry Weather (URG p. 16)

One winter day in Chicago, the low temperature was -6°F. The following day, the low temperature was 16°F. What was the difference in the low temperatures between the two days?

H. Task: Medians and Means (URG p. 17)

Frank's sister, Mary Lou, is a waitress at a restaurant. She keeps track of the tips she receives daily. Here are the total tips she received last week (Monday through Friday): $53.02, $76.39, $20.16, $58.35, and $125.67.

Terry is interested in working at the same restaurant as Mary Lou. She wants to know if the customers tip well. She asks Mary Lou, "On average, do you bring home more or less than $60 a day in tips?" Based on this week's tips, how should Mary Lou answer this question?

Teaching the Activity

There are many references to the plays of William Shakespeare within the text. If students are unfamiliar with Shakespeare, you might say that he is considered by many to be the greatest English playwright of all time. *Hamlet* and *Romeo and Juliet* are two of this author's best-known works.

Page 63

- *How can Howard use the coordinate axes to help him know where the actor might be?*

Howard can use the coordinate axes as guides if he knows the coordinates where the actor will be.

Adventure Book - page 63

Page 64

- *Where is the origin on the grid on the stage floor?*

At the intersection of the two white lines in the center of the stage.

- *What are the two stage hands measuring?*

They are measuring the coordinates for the actor's mark. The actor is 3 meters to the right and 5 meters down from the origin, so the x-coordinate is 3 m and the y-coordinate is -5 m. Point out to students that "left" and "right" are the audience's left and right as they look at the stage. "Up" is toward the back of the stage and "down" is toward the front of the stage.

Adventure Book - page 64

Adventure Book - page 65

Adventure Book - page 66

Page 65

- *In what order should Howard type the coordinates for Hamlet into the computer?*

3, -5

- *Why is it important to type in the coordinates in order?*

If Howard types in -5, 3 instead of 3, -5, the spotlight will be in the wrong place.

Page 66

- *What order should Howard type in these coordinates for Romeo?*

-2, -3

Page 68

- *Why is the spotlight in the wrong place?*

Howard entered the coordinates in the wrong order.

Adventure Book - page 68

Page 69

- *What did Howard do wrong on this page?*

Howard did not enter the negative sign before the 5. The spotlight went to 3 right and 5 up instead of 3 right and 5 down.

Adventure Book - page 69

Adventure Book - page 72

Page 72

• *What do you think will happen in the next scene?*

Students' predictions will vary. Howard may have learned from his mistake in the last scene or he might make a mistake again.

Adventure Book - page 73

Page 73

• *Did Howard enter the correct coordinates?*

No.

• *What coordinates should Howard have entered for Romeo?*

Howard should have entered -2, -3.

Homework and Practice

DPP Bit G provides practice solving problems with negative numbers and DPP Task H reviews averages.

Extension

Have small groups work their way through the story to determine all the errors made by the student, including those he made when trying to compensate for his initial mistakes. Each group is then responsible for illustrating those mistakes for the class. Some groups may wish to use the overhead to explain, while others may choose to do a series of drawings illustrating the spotlight moves.

Language Arts Connection

In the past, several classes chose to rewrite the story as a play and then present it for a group. You may choose to make this a language arts project. A flashlight can serve as the spotlight.

Resource

Shakespeare, William. Edited by David Bevington. *The Complete Works of Shakespeare.* Addison-Wesley, Boston, MA, 1997 (4th ed.).

Lesson 4

Mr. Origin

Lesson Overview

Students map the location of objects in a room (or on the playground) using a four-quadrant coordinate map. They use the map to make predictions about the distance between objects.

Key Content

- Finding coordinates of an object relative to the origin.
- Plotting points using ordered pairs in the four quadrants.
- Making a four-quadrant coordinate map.
- Using a four-quadrant scale map to find distances.

Key Vocabulary

- Mr. Origin

Math Facts

DPP items I and K review the multiplication and division facts for the 2s and the square numbers.

Homework

1. Have students draw a coordinate map of a room in their home.
2. Students complete the *Label the Axes* Homework Page in the *Discovery Assignment Book*.
3. Assign Part 5 of the Home Practice.

Assessment

Use the *Coordinates: Getting to the Point* Assessment Page to assess students' abilities to graph points.

Curriculum Sequence

Before This Unit

Students have used Mr. Origin to develop their understanding of maps and coordinates since first grade. In first and second grade Mr. Origin was positioned on a line to represent the origin, or reference point. Then, students located an object using its distance and direction (front/back or left/right) from Mr. Origin. In first grade, the distance from Mr. Origin to an object was measured in links, and the direction was given as left or right. In second grade, the distance was measured in centimeters, and the direction was given as left, right, front, or back. In third grade Mr. Origin was placed on a flat surface. Then the location of an object was determined by using two numbers, a left/right coordinate and front/back coordinate. Students used only positive coordinates (the first quadrant). They also used a map scale in third grade.

After This Unit

Using a map scale is a type of proportional reasoning. Proportional reasoning is explored in greater depth in Unit 13.

Materials List

Supplies and Copies

Student	Teacher
Supplies for Each Student Group • meterstick or trundle wheel • Mr. Origin, optional • centimeter ruler	**Supplies** • Mr. Origin • 7 index cards to label objects
Copies • 1 copy of *Coordinates: Getting to the Point* per student (*Unit Resource Guide* Page 71) • 2 copies of *Centimeter Grid Paper* per student (*Unit Resource Guide* Page 48) • 1 copy of *Three-column Data Table* per student, optional (*Unit Resource Guide* Page 72)	**Copies/Transparencies**

All blackline masters including assessment, transparency, and DPP masters are also on the Teacher Resource CD.

Student Books
Mr. Origin (*Student Guide* Pages 327–329)
Label the Axes (*Discovery Assignment Book* Page 165)

Daily Practice and Problems and Home Practice
DPP items I–L (*Unit Resource Guide* Pages 17–19)
Home Practice Part 5 (*Discovery Assignment Book* Page 163)

Note: Classrooms whose pacing differs significantly from the suggested pacing of the units should use the Math Facts Calendar in Section 4 of the *Facts Resource Guide* to ensure students receive the complete math facts program.

Daily Practice and Problems

Suggestions for using the DPPs are on page 68.

I. Bit: Dividing by Multiples of Ten (URG p. 17)

A. $2000 \div 100 =$

B. $16{,}000 \div 200 =$

C. $40{,}000 \div 2 =$

D. $160 \div 40 =$

E. $25{,}000 \div 50 =$

F. $80{,}000 \div 40 =$

G. $1400 \div 7 =$

H. $900 \div 3 =$

I. $8100 \div 900 =$

K. Bit: Multiplying and Dividing by Multiples of Ten (URG p. 18)

A. $80 \times 800 =$

B. $60 \times 200 =$

C. $90 \times 200 =$

D. $3600 \div 60 =$

E. $4900 \div 70 =$

F. $10{,}000 \div 50 =$

J. Task: Practice (URG p. 18)

Solve the following using paper and pencil only. Estimate to make sure each answer is reasonable.

A. $832 \times 12 =$

B. $7850 \div 45 =$

C. $2824 - 1586 =$

D. $178 \times 0.3 =$

E. $4758 + 2517 =$

F. $2804 \div 79 =$

L. Task: Fractions (URG p. 19)

1. Use paper and pencil to add or subtract the fractions below. Estimate to be sure your answers are reasonable.

   A. $\frac{3}{8} + \frac{1}{4} =$

   B. $\frac{4}{5} + \frac{2}{3} =$

   C. $\frac{11}{12} - \frac{1}{3} =$

   D. $\frac{8}{9} - \frac{1}{3} =$

   E. $\frac{11}{12} + \frac{1}{6} =$

   F. $\frac{7}{10} - \frac{2}{5} =$

2. Explain your estimation strategy for Question 1E.

Figure 6: *Using Mr. Origin to describe the location of objects in the classroom*

Before the Activity

Set up Mr. Origin and label 6–8 objects in your room that will be mapped with the letters A, B, and so on. You can add a few additional objects to use to practice finding coordinates. Be sure there is at least one labeled object in each quadrant.

> ## TIMS Tip
>
> Students will predict the distance from object A to object B. These two objects should be placed in different quadrants, at least 2 meters apart.
>
> Be sure students are able to distinguish Mr. Origin's right hand from his left. If necessary, tape a piece of paper that is a different color than Mr. Origin on his right arm.
>
> You can use gym tape or ribbon to lay out *x* and *y* axes on the floor.

Teaching the Activity

Part 1 **Introducing Mr. Origin**

Introduce **Mr. Origin** using the *Student Guide.* On a graph, the origin is the point (0, 0). We locate objects on a flat surface (like the floor of a classroom) similar to the way we locate points on a graph. Point out that once we place Mr. Origin at a specific location, we can imagine the *x*-axis running left-right through Mr. Origin's arms and a *y*-axis running front/back through the center of Mr. Origin. Mr. Origin's right arm has an octagon. It points to the positive half of

the *x*-axis. Mr. Origin's button on his front points to the positive half of the *y*-axis. If we covered the floor with graph paper, we could find the coordinates of any object, just as we did in Lesson 2. Since there is no graph paper on the floor, we have to use our imagination and a meterstick to find coordinates of the object.

The data collection part of this activity consists in finding the *x*- and *y*-coordinates of the objects using metric measure. A question that arises is what units to use. A proper tool for measuring distances in the classroom is the meterstick. But, the degree of accuracy we want is not obvious. In general, measurement accuracy is determined by two things:

1. The accuracy of the measurement tool used.
2. The use that is made of the measurement.

In this case, we suggest students make their measurements to the nearest centimeter. Later in the lesson, students will make a scale map and then predict the actual distance between two objects and check their predictions. Using centimeters often makes the calculations necessary for the scale map easier. For this reason, in our examples we show measurements to the nearest centimeter.

Have one of your students find the *x*-coordinate of an object in the classroom by measuring its distance to the right or left of Mr. Origin along the *x*-axis. Then the student should turn toward the object and measure the distance from the *x*-axis to the center of the object, in the *y*-direction (i.e., parallel to the *y*-axis). Note that when we talk about "the coordinates of an object," we really mean the coordinates of the center of the object. For example, in the classroom sketched in Figure 6, with Mr. Origin located as shown, we found that the wastebasket had *x*-coordinate = 200 cm and *y*-coordinate = 100 cm while the teacher's desk had *x*-coordinate = -200 cm and *y*-coordinate = -150 cm. The students measured to the center of the objects. Have students make a quick estimate of their measurements before they measure carefully.

Part 2 Finding Coordinates for Making a Map

Divide students into groups of, at most, three. Then have them collect their data as described in **Question 1** in the *Student Guide*. The data collected by one group of students is shown in Figure 7.

Object	*x*-coordinate in cm	*y*-coordinate in cm
A. wastebasket	200	100
B. Mr. Moreno's desk	-200	-150
C. globe	-490	-460
D. CD player	30	-390
E. round table	-310	120
F. door	120	300

Figure 7: *Mr. Origin data table*

TIMS Tip

Students will be making predictions about distances between some of these objects. If this activity runs into another day, mark where the objects are, so students can check their predictions the next day.

Part 3 Drawing Coordinate Maps

Once the data are collected, students draw their maps *(Question 2)*. Students first decide on a map scale to use. The simplest scale is one in which 1 cm represents 100 cm or 1 cm represents 1 m. An improper choice of scale can result in a map that does not fit on the graph paper or a map that is too small to be useful. Our objects were within an 8 m × 10 m space, so all the objects fit nicely on the graph paper. If your space is similar, you can use the same scale.

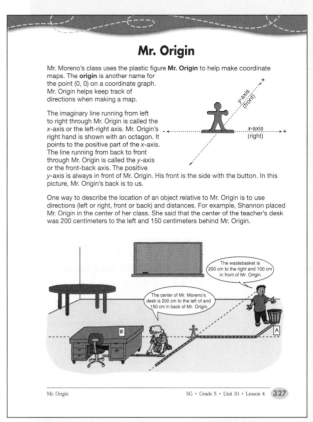

Student Guide - page 327

Instead of using directions like left and right, mathematicians and scientists use positive and negative numbers. They have agreed that on the *x*-axis, right is positive and left is negative. On the *y*-axis front (or forward) is positive and back is negative.

Shannon translated her work into scientific language. She said that the *x*-coordinate of the teacher's desk was -200 centimeters and the *y*-coordinate was -150 centimeters.

Finding Coordinates Relative to Mr. Origin

• You and your classmates will use Mr. Origin to help make a map of your classroom or your playground. First, place Mr. Origin somewhere in the area to be mapped. Your teacher may have placed Mr. Origin for you.
• The class or your teacher will choose some objects in the classroom to be mapped. Each object should be labeled with a letter of the alphabet.

1. Work with your group to find the coordinates of each object. Measure to the center of each object. Record your data in a table like the one at the right. Measure to the nearest centimeter.

Object	*x*-coordinate in cm	*y*-coordinate in cm
A.		
B.		
C.		
D.		
E.		
F.		

Making a Map

• You will need a sheet of *Centimeter Grid Paper* to make your map. Look at your data points. Decide where you need to draw the coordinate axes so that all the points will fit. Label the *x*-axis and the *y*-axis. Look at your data points and decide what scale you should use.
• Discuss with your group how to number the axes on your map.
• Decide on the scale for your map.

2. Plot the points from your data table on your map.

Student Guide - page 328 (Answers on p. 73)

Content Note

Scale Maps. The symbol : can be read as "represents." For example 1 cm : 100 cm can be read as "one centimeter (on the map) represents 100 centimeters (in the real world)." When mapping it is important to use the same scale on the horizontal and vertical axes. Choosing different scales on the axes will result in a distorted map and will make the map useless for finding diagonal distances.

Our map is shown in Figure 8. We plot a point to locate the center of each object. The objects are sketched in afterward. To sketch an object properly, one needs to know the dimensions of the object. For example, the desk is a little less than 100 cm or 1 m wide and about 150 cm or 1.5 m long; the wastebasket is about 50 cm in diameter. A second version of the map is shown in Figure 9. In this map, the scale is 1 cm : 50 cm. We turned the paper sideways to fit all the points. For this map, we used a plain piece of *Centimeter Grid Paper* and sketched in the axes.

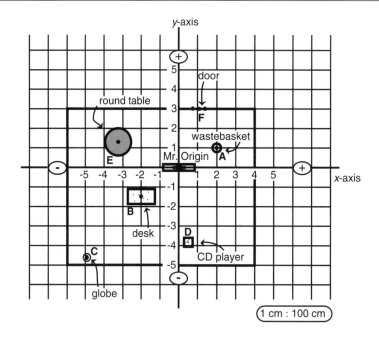

Figure 8: *Classroom map with scale of 1 cm : 100 cm*

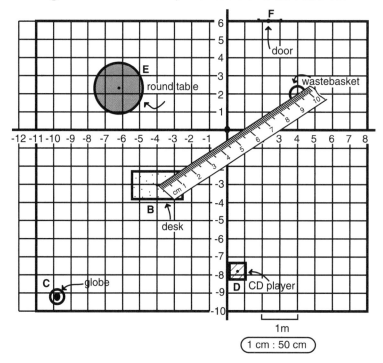

Figure 9: *Classroom map with scale of 1 cm : 50 cm*

Part 4 Using Coordinate Maps

For **Question 3,** students predict the distance between two objects. (The distances are measured "as the crow flies.") On our data table in Figure 7, object A is the wastebasket and object B is Mr. Moreno's desk. Measuring on our map in Figure 9, we get a distance of 9.5 cm. Have students measure the distance between object A and B on their maps. Then ask them how they can convert the map measurement in centimeters to the actual distance the two objects are from each other. Possible strategies using our measurements include:

- The map scale tells me that 1 cm represents 50 cm. That means 2 cm represents 100 cm. I skip counted along my ruler. For every 2 cm I counted 100 real centimeters. 100, 200, 300, 400 centimeters. One more centimeter on the map gives us 450 cm in our classroom. Finally, if 1 cm on the map represents 50 cm, then 0.5 cm on the map represents 25 cm. So 9.5 cm on our map represents 475 cm in our classroom.

- The map scale tells us that 1 cm represents 50 cm. Each centimeter on the map represents 50 centimeters in the classroom. Since we measured 9.5 centimeters, we can multiply 9.5 × 50 to get a predicted distance of 475 cm.

In **Questions 4A** and **4B** students measure the actual distance between object A and object B in their classroom and find the difference between the actual distance and the prediction they made in **Question 3.** Then in **Question 4C** students decide if the prediction is close. Students should understand that if the objects are close to one another, the error should be smaller than if the objects are far apart.

In **Question 4D** students determine if the difference or error is less than 10% of the actual distance. If, for example, the measured distance is 490 cm, the error or the difference between the predicted and measured distance is 15 cm. An error of 15 cm out of a measured 490 cm is less than 10% since 10% of 490 cm is 49 cm. **Omit *Question 4D* if students did not complete Unit 2 Lesson 4 *How Close Is Close Enough?***

We provide a coordinate map of a playground in **Question 5** and ask students to find the distance between a flagpole and a slide. A good eyeball estimate of the map distance is between 4 cm and 6 cm. Measuring with a ruler, we find the distance is 5.0 cm, so the actual distance is 1500 cm or 15 m.

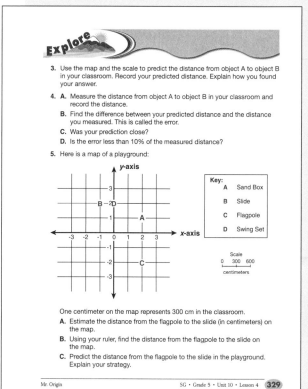

Student Guide - page 329 *(Answers on p. 73)*

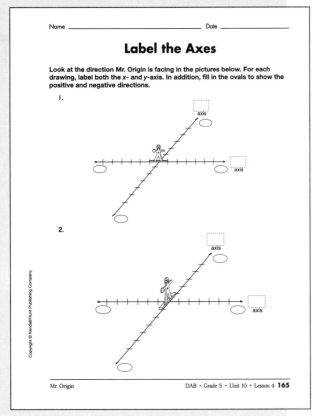

Discovery Assignment Book - page 165 *(Answers on p. 74)*

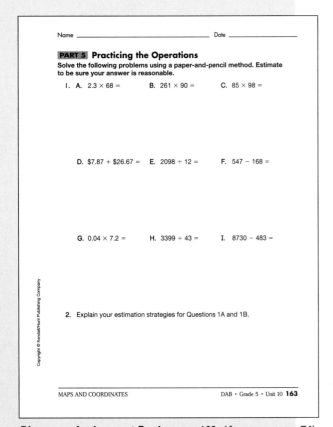

Discovery Assignment Book - page 163 *(Answers on p. 74)*

DPP items I and K review the multiplication and division facts for the 2s and the square numbers using multiples of ten.

- Have students draw a coordinate map of a room in their home. The origin should be near the center of the room. Measurements can be made in centimeters. If students do not have a ruler or meterstick at home, they can estimate using the length of a body part (e.g., a foot) or the length of a sheet of paper (e.g., an $8\frac{1}{2}$-inch-by-11-inch piece of paper is about 21cm by 28 cm).

- Assign DPP Tasks J and L for homework. Item J practices computation with whole numbers and decimals. Item L practices addition and subtraction with fractions.

- Have students complete the *Label the Axes* Homework Page in the *Discovery Assignment Book*. It includes perspective drawings of Mr. Origin and asks students to label the axes. This is a bit tricky since Mr. Origin may be facing in a direction the student is not used to. In the first drawing, the positive *x*-direction is to our left (Mr. Origin's right) and the positive *y*-direction is toward us.

- Assign Part 5 of the Home Practice, which provides practice with computation.

Answers for Part 5 of the Home Practice are in the Answer Key at the end of this lesson and at the end of this unit.

Use the *Coordinates: Getting to the Point* Assessment Page in the *Unit Resource Guide* to assess students' abilities to graph points.

Changing the Origin. Use the same objects you used in the lesson; however, this time use more than one Mr. Origin. Place each Mr. Origin in a different location and position. Assign one Mr. Origin to each group. Tell students that each group will once again measure to find the *x*-coordinate and *y*-coordinate of each object and make a map. When groups complete their maps, ask:

- *Is your group's data the same as another group's with a different Mr. Origin? Explain why or why not.* (When we move Mr. Origin, the coordinate system moves with him. Some students may notice that even though the coordinates change, the map looks similar, with the same scale. The map may be translated or rotated, however.)

- *Would your data be the same if you kept your Mr. Origin in the same spot but turned him around so he faces the opposite direction? Explain why or why not.* (The measurements are all the same, but the direction changes. Left and right are interchanged as are front and back. This means the negative coordinates become positive and vice-versa.)

Drawing a Scale Map. Give students the coordinates (in cm) of several cities in the imaginary state of Sionilli.

City	Coordinates in cm
Appleville	(4, -3)
Baytown	(-6, 0)
Centerburg	(5, 5)
Dense City	(-2, 8)

They must first draw a scale map locating the cities using a scale in which 1 cm represents 100 miles. Then they find the distances between each pair of cities. Imagine there are no roads in this state and you have the job of building enough roads to get from any city to any other city. All roads can be straight lines (there are no hills in Sionilli). The currency in Sionilli is the rallod. It costs 100,000 rallods to build one mile of road. Design a road system for Sionilli that will allow you to get from any city to any other. What will it cost to build those roads? Try to spend as little money as possible.

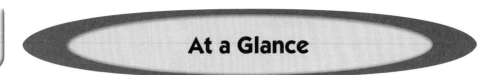

At a Glance

Math Facts and Daily Practice and Problems

DPP items I and K review the multiplication and division facts for the 2s and the square numbers. Tasks J and L practice estimation and computation with whole numbers, decimals, and fractions.

Part 1. Introducing Mr. Origin

1. Use the *Student Guide* Activity Pages to introduce Mr. Origin.
2. Position Mr. Origin in your classroom. Label objects in the classroom.
3. Select students to demonstrate how to find coordinates of an object by measuring its distance from Mr. Origin.

Part 2. Finding Coordinates for Making a Map

Students find coordinates of objects that you select and label and enter coordinates in a data table. *(Question 1)*

Part 3. Drawing Coordinate Maps

Students draw a scale map of the objects in the room. *(Question 2)*

Part 4. Using Coordinate Maps

1. Students use the coordinate map to predict the distance between two objects. Students check their predictions by measuring the actual distance. *(Questions 3–4)*
2. Students complete *Question 5* in the *Student Guide.*

Homework

1. Have students draw a coordinate map of a room in their home.
2. Students complete the *Label the Axes* Homework Page in the *Discovery Assignment Book.*
3. Assign Part 5 of the Home Practice.

Assessment

Use the *Coordinates: Getting to the Point* Assessment Page to assess students' abilities to graph points.

Extension

1. Using the same objects as in the lesson, place other Mr. Origins in different locations and positions. Assign each group a Mr. Origin to use to make a map. Have students examine the diffferent maps and discuss similarities and differences.
2. Give students coordinates and have them make a scale map.

Answer Key is on pages 73–75.

Notes:

Coordinates: Getting to the Point

On the grid below, draw the triangle, circle, heart, and square at the coordinates given.

	Object	*x*-coordinate	*y*-coordinate	Ordered Pair
I.	▲	3	-2	
2.	●	-1	-4	
3.	♥	5	4	
4.	■	-6	4	

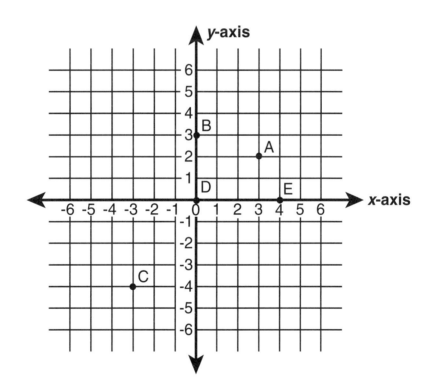

Name the coordinates of points A, B, C, D, and E.

5. A _____

6. B _____

7. C _____

8. D _____

9. E _____

Name _____   Date _____

_____

Three-column Data Table, Blackline Master

Student Guide (p. 328)

1. See Figure 7 in Lesson Guide 4 for a sample data table.*

2. See Figures 8 and 9 in Lesson Guide 4 for two sample maps.*

See Lesson Guide 4 for sample answers to *Questions 3* and *4,* which are based on the sample map in Figure 9.*

Instead of using directions like left and right, mathematicians and scientists use positive and negative numbers. They have agreed that on the x-axis, right is positive and left is negative. On the y-axis front (or forward) is positive and back is negative.

Shannon translated her work into scientific language. She said that the x-coordinate of the teacher's desk was -200 centimeters and the y-coordinate was -150 centimeters.

Finding Coordinates Relative to Mr. Origin
- You and your classmates will use Mr. Origin to help make a map of your classroom or your playground. First, place Mr. Origin somewhere in the area to be mapped. Your teacher may have placed Mr. Origin for you.
- The class or your teacher will choose some objects in the classroom to be mapped. Each object should be labeled with a letter of the alphabet.

Collect

1. Work with your group to find the coordinates of each object. Measure to the center of each object. Record your data in a table like the one at the right. Measure to the nearest centimeter.

Object	x-coordinate in cm	y-coordinate in cm
A.		
B.		
C.		
D.		
E.		
F.		

Making a Map
- You will need a sheet of *Centimeter Grid Paper* to make your map. Look at your data points. Decide where you need to draw the coordinate axes so that all the points will fit. Label the x-axis and the y-axis. Look at your data points and decide what scale you should use.
- Discuss with your group how to number the axes on your map.
- Decide on the scale for your map.

2. Plot the points from your data table on your map.

328 SG • Grade 5 • Unit 10 • Lesson 4   Mr. Origin

Student Guide - page 328

Student Guide (p. 329)

3. Answers will vary.*

4.* A. Answers will vary.
    B. Answers will vary.
    C. Answers will vary.
    D. Answers will vary.

5.* A. 4–6 cm
    B. 5 cm
    C. $5 \times 300 = 1500$ cm

Explore

3. Use the map and the scale to predict the distance from object A to object B in your classroom. Record your predicted distance. Explain how you found your answer.

4. A. Measure the distance from object A to object B in your classroom and record the distance.
    B. Find the difference between your predicted distance and the distance you measured. This is called the error.
    C. Was your prediction close?
    D. Is the error less than 10% of the measured distance?

5. Here is a map of a playground:

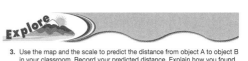

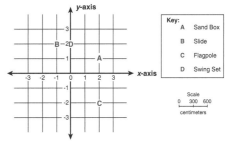

Key:
A   Sand Box
B   Slide
C   Flagpole
D   Swing Set

Scale
0   300   600
centimeters

One centimeter on the map represents 300 cm in the classroom.
    A. Estimate the distance from the flagpole to the slide (in centimeters) on the map.
    B. Using your ruler, find the distance from the flagpole to the slide on the map.
    C. Predict the distance from the flagpole to the slide in the playground. Explain your strategy.

Mr. Origin   SG • Grade 5 • Unit 10 • Lesson 4 **329**

Student Guide - page 329

*Answers and/or discussion are included in the Lesson Guide.

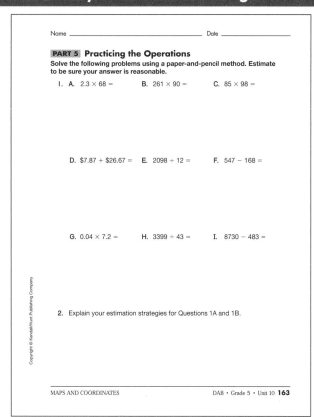

Discovery Assignment Book - page 163

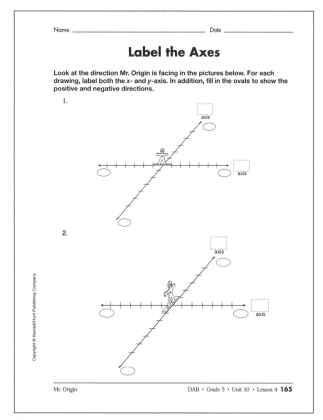

Discovery Assignment Book - page 165

Discovery Assignment Book (p. 163)

Home Practice*

Part 5. Practicing the Operations

1. **A.** 156.40   **B.** 23,490
   C. 8330   **D.** $34.54
   E. 174 R10   **F.** 379
   G. 0.288   **H.** 79 R2
   I. 8247

2. **A.** Answers will vary. Possible response:
   $2 \times 70 = 140$

   B. Answers will vary:
   $260 \times 100 = 26,000$

Discovery Assignment Book (p. 165)

Label the Axes

1.†

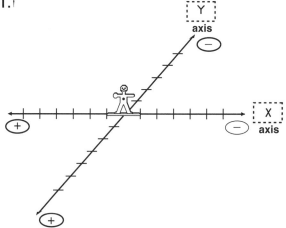

2.

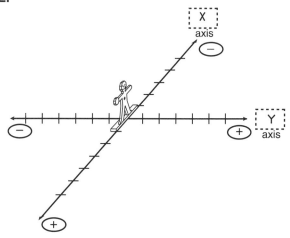

*Answers for all the Home Practice in the *Discovery Assignment Book* are at the end of the unit.

†Answers and/or discussion are included in the Lesson Guide.

Unit Resource Guide (p. 71)

Coordinates: Getting to the Point

1. (3, -2)
2. (-1, -4)
3. (5, 4)
4. (-6, 4)

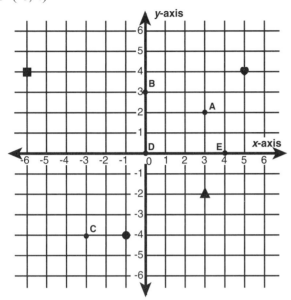

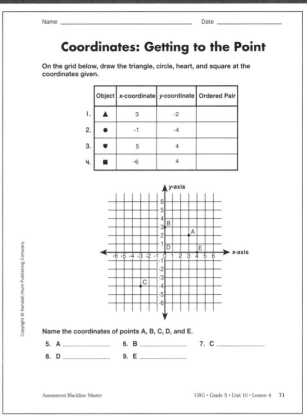

Unit Resource Guide - page 71

5. (3, 2)
6. (0, 3)
7. (-3, -4)
8. (0, 0)
9. (4, 0)

Lesson 5

Plotting Shapes

Estimated Class Sessions

1

Lesson Overview

Students plot points in four quadrants and then connect the points to form shapes.

Key Content

- Plotting points using ordered pairs in four quadrants.
- Graphing shapes in four quadrants.

Homework

1. Students design their own shape in *Question 5,* which can be assigned for homework.
2. Assign Part 4 of the Home Practice.

Assessment

Assess students' abilities to plot points as they complete *Questions 1–3.* Record your observations on the *Observational Assessment Record.*

Materials List

Supplies and Copies

Student	Teacher
Supplies for Each Student	**Supplies**
Copies • several copies of *Four-Quadrant Grid Paper* per student (*Unit Resource Guide* Page 47) • several copies of *Half-Centimeter Graph Paper* per student (*Unit Resource Guide* Page 83)	**Copies/Transparencies** • 1 transparency of *Four-Quadrant Grid Paper* (*Unit Resource Guide* Page 47) • 1 transparency of *Half-Centimeter Graph Paper,* optional (*Unit Resource Guide* Page 83)

All blackline masters including assessment, transparency, and DPP masters are also on the Teacher Resource CD.

Student Books
Plotting Shapes (*Student Guide* Pages 330–331)

Daily Practice and Problems and Home Practice
DPP items M–N (*Unit Resource Guide* Pages 19–20)
Home Practice Part 4 (*Discovery Assignment Book* Page 162)

Note: Classrooms whose pacing differs significantly from the suggested pacing of the units should use the Math Facts Calendar in Section 4 of the *Facts Resource Guide* to ensure students receive the complete math facts program.

Assessment Tools
Observational Assessment Record (*Unit Resource Guide* Pages 11–12)

M. Bit: What's the Probability (URG p. 19)

Roberto rolls a number cube. The six faces show the numbers 1, 2, 3, 4, 5, and 6. What's the probability that he will roll:

A. a number less than 3?

B. an odd number?

N. Challenge: Coordinates
(URG p. 20)

Use a piece of graph paper. Scale the horizontal and vertical axes by ones up to 10.

The midpoint of a line segment divides the line into two equal halves. The midpoint O of the line segment LM is at (6, 4). The endpoint M has coordinates (10, 5). Plot O and M. What are the coordinates of the endpoint L?

Teaching the Activity

Students draw shapes using ordered pairs as vertices (corners). This is similar to the familiar primary grade activity of "connect the dots." However, now students have to plot the dots first.

Discuss the introduction on the *Plotting Shapes* Activity Pages in the *Student Guide.* José takes Shape Orders that consist of ordered pairs. He plots these points and then connects the points in the order listed to make shapes. Do the example Shape Order with the class on the overhead projector using a transparency of *Four-Quadrant Grid Paper.*

Questions 1–3 give students a chance to draw shapes on *Four-Quadrant Grid Paper* or other graph paper. Before a student continues, make sure he or she has plotted the points and drawn the shapes correctly.

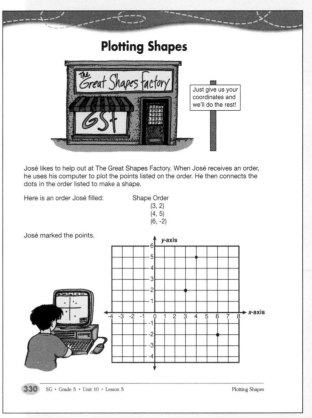

Student Guide - page 330

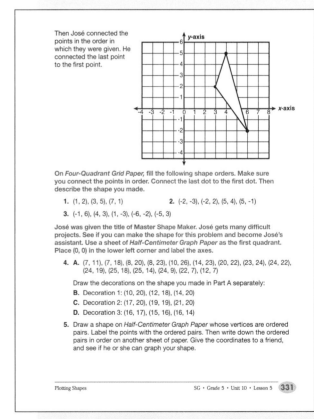

Student Guide - page 331 *(Answers on p. 84)*

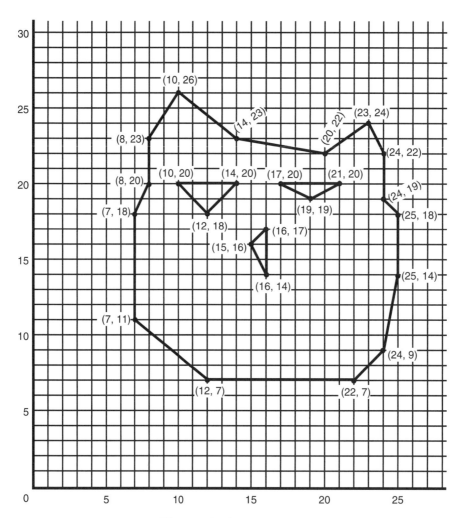

Figure 10: *Graphing a cat*

Question 4 is a complicated figure to be done on *Half-Centimeter Graph Paper.* It is best to use the entire sheet as the first quadrant. Thus the lower left hand corner of the grid is (0, 0). None of the ordered pairs has a negative coordinate. The resulting shape is a picture of a cat's head. The three decorations form two eyes and the nose as shown in Figure 10. As an extension, ask students to draw whiskers on the cat and then give the coordinates of the points that need to be connected.

Question 5 asks students to make up their own shapes. They draw a shape on *Half-Centimeter Graph Paper.* The shape should consist of straight lines. They then record the ordered pairs on paper, in order. Tell students it does not matter which point they choose to begin the list. Students then exchange lists and each person draws the shape from the ordered pairs they were given. Students should compare drawings to make sure the original and the new drawing are the same. If they are not, they should find any mistakes. You can assign parts of this problem as homework.

TIMS Tip

Make sure you emphasize to students the importance of connecting the dots in the order in which they are listed.

Homework and Practice

- Assign parts of *Question 5* in the *Student Guide* as homework.

- DPP Bit M provides practice with probability concepts.

- Assign Part 4 of the Home Practice, which reviews the order of operations.

Answers for Part 4 of the Home Practice are in the Answer Key at the end of this lesson and at the end of this unit.

Assessment

Observe students as they complete *Questions 1–3.* Record your observations on the *Observational Assessment Record.*

Extension

- If you have large graph paper, students can graph complicated shapes to make a display.

- Ask students to draw whiskers on the cat in *Question 4.* They should then list the coordinates of the points needed to make the whiskers.

- Assign DPP Challenge N, which involves graphing, coordinates, and midpoints of lines.

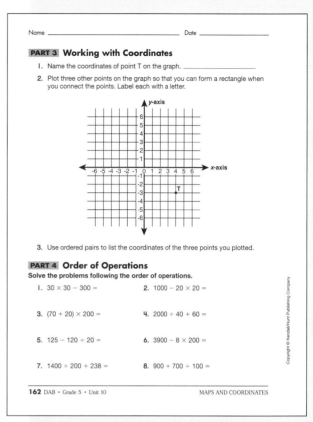

Name _____ Date _____

PART 3 Working with Coordinates

1. Name the coordinates of point T on the graph. _____

2. Plot three other points on the graph so that you can form a rectangle when you connect the points. Label each with a letter.

3. Use ordered pairs to list the coordinates of the three points you plotted.

PART 4 Order of Operations

Solve the problems following the order of operations.

1. $30 \times 30 - 300 =$ 2. $1000 - 20 \times 20 =$

3. $(70 + 20) \times 200 =$ 4. $2000 \div 40 + 60 =$

5. $125 - 120 \div 20 =$ 6. $3900 - 8 \times 200 =$

7. $1400 \div 200 + 238 =$ 8. $900 + 700 \div 100 =$

162 DAB • Grade 5 • Unit 10   MAPS AND COORDINATES

Discovery Assignment Book - page 162 *(Answers on p. 85)*

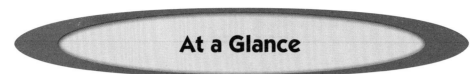

At a Glance

Math Facts and Daily Practice and Problems

DPP items M and N involve probability and coordinate geometry.

Teaching the Activity

1. Use the *Plotting Shapes* Activity Pages in the *Student Guide* to discuss José's job of drawing shapes on the computer. José first plots the points and then connects the points in the order they are given.
2. Students plot points, connect points, and draw shapes on *Four-Quadrant Grid Paper. (Questions 1–3)*
3. Students draw the shape in *Question 4* on *Half-Centimeter Graph Paper.*

Homework

1. Students design their own shape in *Question 5,* which can be assigned for homework.
2. Assign Part 4 of the Home Practice.

Assessment

Assess students' abilities to plot points as they complete *Questions 1–3.* Record your observations on the *Observational Assessment Record.*

Extension

1. Use large graph paper for students to graph complicated shapes.
2. Have students draw whiskers and write the coordinates for the cat in *Question 4.*
3. Assign DPP Challenge N.

Answer Key is on pages 84–85.

Notes:

Name _____ Date _____

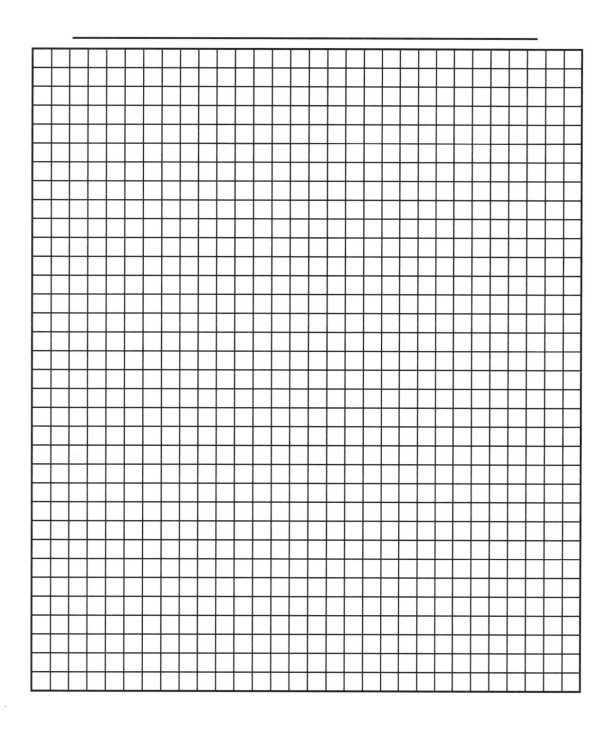

Half-Centimeter Graph Paper, Blackline Master

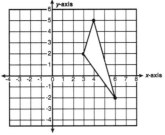

Then José connected the points in the order in which they were given. He connected the last point to the first point.

On *Four-Quadrant Grid Paper,* fill the following shape orders. Make sure you connect the points in order. Connect the last dot to the first dot. Then describe the shape you made.

1. (1, 2), (3, 5), (7, 1) **2.** (-2, -3), (-2, 2), (5, 4), (5, -1)

3. (-1, 6), (4, 3), (1, -3), (-6, -2), (-5, 3)

José was given the title of Master Shape Maker. José gets many difficult projects. See if you can make the shape for this problem and become José's assistant. Use a sheet of *Half-Centimeter Graph Paper* as the first quadrant. Place (0, 0) in the lower left corner and label the axes.

4. A. (7, 11), (7, 18), (8, 20), (8, 23), (10, 26), (14, 23), (20, 22), (23, 24), (24, 22), (24, 19), (25, 18), (25, 14), (24, 9), (22, 7), (12, 7)

Draw the decorations on the shape you made in Part A separately:

B. Decoration 1: (10, 20), (12, 18), (14, 20)
C. Decoration 2: (17, 20), (19, 19), (21, 20)
D. Decoration 3: (16, 17), (15, 16), (16, 14)

5. Draw a shape on *Half-Centimeter Graph Paper* whose vertices are ordered pairs. Label the points with the ordered pairs. Then write down the ordered pairs in order on another sheet of paper. Give the coordinates to a friend, and see if he or she can graph your shape.

Plotting Shapes   SG • Grade 5 • Unit 10 • Lesson 5   **331**

Student Guide - **page 331**

Student Guide (p. 331)

1. Triangle

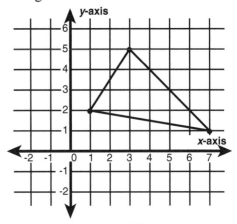

2. Parallelogram or quadrilateral

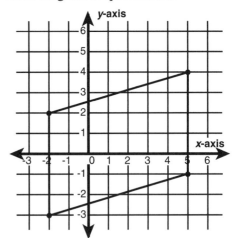

3. Pentagon

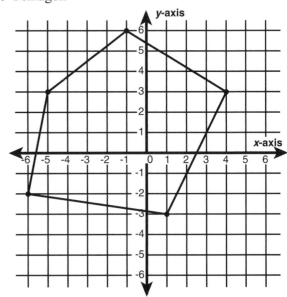

4. See Figure 10 in Lesson Guide 5.*

5. Answers will vary.

*Answers and/or discussion are included in the Lesson Guide.

Discovery Assignment Book (p. 162)

Home Practice*

Part 4. Order of Operations

1. 600
2. 600
3. 18,000
4. 110
5. 119
6. 2300
7. 245
8. 907

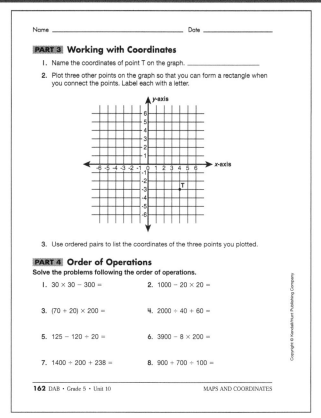

Name _____ Date _____

PART 3 **Working with Coordinates**

1. Name the coordinates of point T on the graph. _____

2. Plot three other points on the graph so that you can form a rectangle when you connect the points. Label each with a letter.

3. Use ordered pairs to list the coordinates of the three points you plotted.

PART 4 **Order of Operations**
Solve the problems following the order of operations.

1. $30 \times 30 - 300 =$ 2. $1000 - 20 \times 20 =$

3. $(70 + 20) \times 200 =$ 4. $2000 \div 40 + 60 =$

5. $125 - 120 \div 20 =$ 6. $3900 - 8 \times 200 =$

7. $1400 \div 200 + 238 =$ 8. $900 + 700 \div 100 =$

162 DAB · Grade 5 · Unit 10   MAPS AND COORDINATES

Discovery Assignment Book - page 162

*Answers for all the Home Practice in the *Discovery Assignment Book* are at the end of the unit.

These Boots Are Made for Sliding

Lesson Overview

Estimated Class Sessions

1

Children explore slides (translations) on the Cartesian coordinate system.

Key Content

- Using slides to move shapes about the coordinate system.
- Determining the image of a slide.

Key Vocabulary

- congruent
- corresponding parts
- image
- parallel
- slide

Homework

Assign the homework problems in the *Student Guide*.

Materials List

Supplies and Copies

Student	Teacher
Supplies for Each Student	**Supplies**
Copies • several copies of *Four-Quadrant Grid Paper* per student (*Unit Resource Guide* Page 47) or several copies of *Centimeter Grid Paper* per student with axes drawn (*Unit Resource Guide* Page 48) • 1 copy of *Four-column Data Table* per student (*Unit Resource Guide* Page 94)	**Copies/Transparencies** • 1 transparency of *Four-Quadrant Grid Paper* (*Unit Resource Guide* Page 47) • 1 transparency of *Slides,* optional (*Discovery Assignment Book* Pages 167–171)

All blackline masters including assessment, transparency, and DPP masters are also on the Teacher Resource CD.

Student Books

These Boots Are Made for Sliding (*Student Guide* Pages 332–336)
Slides (*Discovery Assignment Book* Pages 167–171)

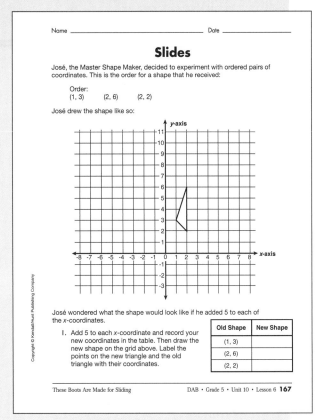

Discovery Assignment Book - page 167 *(Answers on p. 98)*

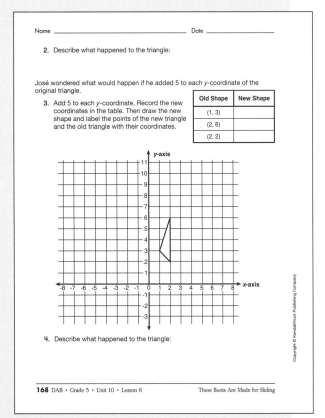

Discovery Assignment Book - page 168 *(Answers on p. 98)*

Teaching the Activity

Part 1 Sliding Along

This activity investigates slides. Mathematically, a **slide** is a motion in the plane that moves every point of a figure a specified distance along a straight line. Children need not learn the mathematical definition. It is more important for them to develop a conceptual understanding of the idea. Note that slides do not allow any rotations of the figure. The new figure is called the **image** of the original figure. Two examples of slides are given in Figure 11. Triangle A′B′C′ is the image of triangle ABC. The matching (corresponding) sides of the figure are parallel (e.g., AB is parallel to A′B′). It is customary to use A′ (read A prime) as the image of A. This makes it clear that A and A′ are **corresponding parts.**

Use the *Slides* Activity Pages in the *Discovery Assignment Book* to begin the discussion. Students can complete the questions independently or in groups. Then discuss the problems together as a class. *Questions 1–2* ask students to investigate what happens when 5 is added to each *x*-coordinate. Students should see that the triangle moves over or slides 5 units to the right. The triangle does not change in shape or size; that is to say, the old triangle and the new triangle are congruent. *Questions 3–4* ask children to investigate what happens when 5 is added to each *y*-coordinate. They should see that the figure slides 5 units forward or up.

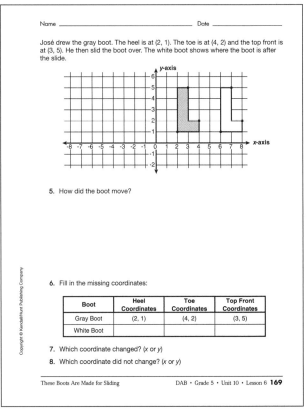

Discovery Assignment Book - page 169 *(Answers on p. 99)*

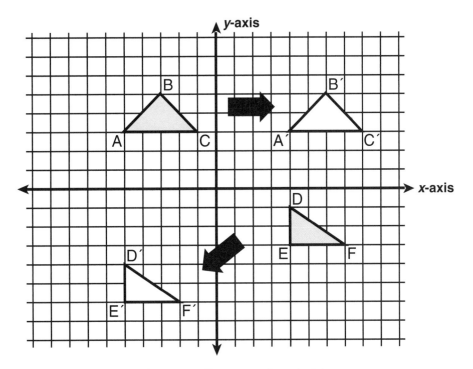

Figure 11: *Two examples of slides*

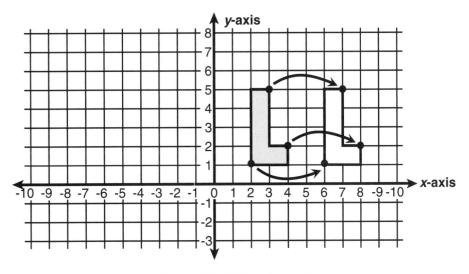

Figure 12: *Sliding four units*

Questions 5–8 ask students to investigate a horizontal slide to the right. Students should see that the boot slid 4 units right as illustrated in Figure 12. The *x*-coordinates of the marked points changed (added 4 to each coordinate). The *y*-coordinates remained the same. At first glance, many students think that the boot slid 2 units, i.e., the space between the gray boot and the white boot. Focus their attention on the original heel and then the new heel.

Content Note

If we are thinking of Mr. Origin as in Lesson 4, boots slide right/left/forward/backward. If we are looking at the coordinate axes, then we say right/left/up/down. Either keep the Mr. Origin terminology or use the standard terminology. For readability, we use up and down here.

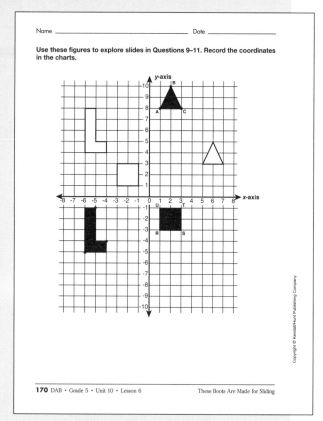

Discovery Assignment Book - page 170

In the image (page 170):

Use these figures to explore slides in Questions 9–11. Record the coordinates in the charts.

y-axis

x-axis

170 DAB • Grade 5 • Unit 10 • Lesson 6   These Boots Are Made for Sliding

---

(page 171 content):

9. The black boot shows the starting position.

Boot	Heel Coordinates	Toe Coordinates	Top Front Coordinates
Black Boot			
White Boot			

Explain how the coordinates changed.

10. The black triangle shows the starting position.

Triangle	Vertex A Coordinates	Vertex B Coordinates	Vertex C Coordinates
Black Triangle			
White Triangle			

Explain how the coordinates changed.

11. The black square shows the starting position.

Square	Vertex R Coordinates	Vertex S Coordinates	Vertex T Coordinates	Vertex U Coordinates
Black Square				
White Square				

Explain how the coordinates changed.

These Boots Are Made for Sliding   DAB • Grade 5 • Unit 10 • Lesson 6 **171**

Discovery Assignment Book - page 171 *(Answers on p. 99)*

In **Questions 9–11,** more slides are investigated. Students should note that for **Question 9,** the boot slid 9 units forward or up. To slide 9 units up means the *y*-coordinates of the new white boot are 9 more than the *y*-coordinates of the black boot. The triangle **(Question 10)** slid 5 units down, 4 units right. Students should see that the *x*-coordinates of the white triangle are 4 more than the *x*-coordinates of the black triangle. The *y*-coordinates of the white triangle are 5 less than the *y*-coordinates of the black triangle. It does not matter whether you slide up/down or right/left first. In **Question 11,** the *x*-coordinates decrease by 4 and the *y*-coordinates increase by 4 when sliding from the black square to the white square.

Discuss with students that slides do not change shapes. The beginning shape and the ending shape are the same; in other words, they are **congruent.** It is important for children to be aware that slides preserve congruence.

Have students complete the Sliding Along section on the *These Boots Are Made for Sliding* Activity Pages in the *Student Guide.* It is best to work in groups on this activity so students discuss the problems. The problems pull together the previous work on slides.

Discuss the term "image": the figure that is the result of a slide. Discuss the matching (or corresponding) parts of an original figure and the image. Discuss the matching vertices, line segments, and angles. For example, the heel of the image boot corresponds to the

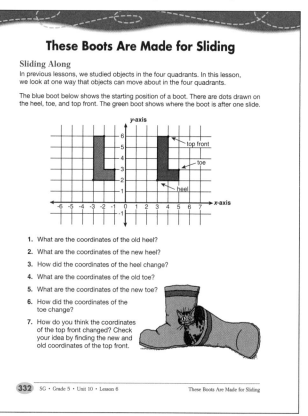

These Boots Are Made for Sliding

Sliding Along
In previous lessons, we studied objects in the four quadrants. In this lesson, we look at one way that objects can move about in the four quadrants.

The blue boot below shows the starting position of a boot. There are dots drawn on the heel, toe, and top front. The green boot shows where the boot is after one slide.

y-axis

top front

toe

heel

x-axis

1. What are the coordinates of the old heel?

2. What are the coordinates of the new heel?

3. How did the coordinates of the heel change?

4. What are the coordinates of the old toe?

5. What are the coordinates of the new toe?

6. How did the coordinates of the toe change?

7. How do you think the coordinates of the top front changed? Check your idea by finding the new and old coordinates of the top front.

332 SG • Grade 5 • Unit 10 • Lesson 6   These Boots Are Made for Sliding

Student Guide - page 332 *(Answers on p. 95)*

heel of the original boot and the bottom of the image boot corresponds to the bottom of the original boot.

Another property of slides is that corresponding sides are **parallel.** For example, focus students' attention on the two triangles for *Questions 8–11.* Ask students what they notice about segments AB and A'B'. If the segments were extended into lines, would they ever meet? Then discuss the fact that all the corresponding sides are parallel.

Part 2 Patterns with Slides

When performing repeated slides, the coordinates form a pattern that can be used to predict the coordinates of figures that are off the graph paper.

Questions 12–15 ask students to investigate repeated slides of a boot and find the pattern. By using the chart, they should be able to predict that 16 slides are needed for the heel to be at (64, 0). Use a *Four-column Data Table* for *Question 13.*

Questions 16–19 ask students to draw a boot and then discover how the boot slides.

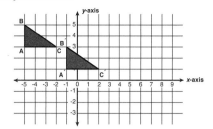

The purple triangle shows where the triangle starts. The red triangle shows where the triangle is after one slide.

8. Describe how the triangle moved.
9. How did the x-coordinates change?
10. How did the y-coordinates change?

When all the points of an object move the same distance in the same direction, the movement is called a **slide.** Triangle A'B'C' (read A prime, B prime, C prime), the new shape, is called the **image** of triangle ABC. Matching parts of the shape such as Sides AB and A'B' are **corresponding parts.** Vertex A and Vertex A' are corresponding parts too.

11. Name four more pairs of corresponding parts (sides or vertices).

These Boots Are Made for Sliding   SG • Grade 5 • Unit 10 • Lesson 6   **333**

Student Guide - page 333 (Answers on p. 95)

Patterns with Slides
The orange boot below shows the starting position. The yellow boot shows where the boot is after one slide. The boot slides again. The red boot shows where the boot is after the second slide.

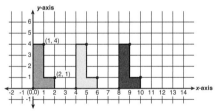

12. Describe how this boot moved.

13. Imagine that the boot follows the same pattern for each slide. Use a *Four-column Data Table* to complete the table.

Slide	Heel Coordinates	Toe Coordinates	Top Front Coordinates
0	(0, 0)	(2, 1)	(1, 4)
1	?	?	(5, 4)
2	?	(10, 1)	?
3	(12, 0)	?	?
4	?	(18, 1)	?
10	?	?	(41, 4)

14. Explain what you did to find the answers in the table.

15. If the heel is at (64, 0), then how many slides has the boot made?

334 SG • Grade 5 • Unit 10 • Lesson 6   These Boots Are Made for Sliding

Student Guide - page 334 (Answers on p. 96)

---

16. In this question, we will study a different boot and a different slide. Use the first row (Slide 0) of the chart to draw the boot on a piece of *Four-Quadrant Grid Paper.* Shade this boot.

Slide	Heel Coordinates	Toe Coordinates	Top Front Coordinates
0	(5, 3)	(7, 4)	(6, 7)
1	(2, 1)	(4, 2)	(3, 5)
2	?	?	?
3	?	?	?
4	?	?	?
5	?	?	?
10	?	?	?

17. Use the second row of the chart in Question 16 to draw the new boot.

18. Fill in the rest of the chart in Question 16.

19. Explain how the boot in Question 16 slides.

Homework

For each shape on the following grid, describe the slide needed to move the purple figure onto its image, the pink figure. How many units to the right or left and up or down is the slide?

1. Parallelogram
2. Triangle
3. Pentagon
4. Rectangle

These Boots Are Made for Sliding   SG • Grade 5 • Unit 10 • Lesson 6   **335**

Student Guide - page 335 (Answers on pp. 96–97)

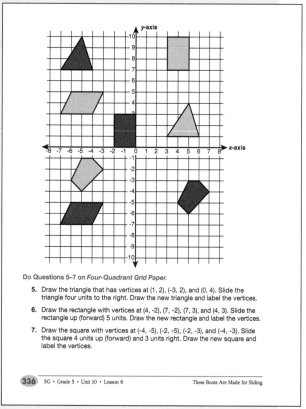

Do Questions 5–7 on *Four-Quadrant Grid Paper.*

5. Draw the triangle that has vertices at (1, 2), (-3, 2), and (0, 4). Slide the triangle four units to the right. Draw the new triangle and label the vertices.

6. Draw the rectangle with vertices at (4, -2), (7, -2), (7, 3), and (4, 3). Slide the rectangle up (forward) 5 units. Draw the new rectangle and label the vertices.

7. Draw the square with vertices at (-4, -5), (-2, -5), (-2, -3), and (-4, -3). Slide the square 4 units up (forward) and 3 units right. Draw the new square and label the vertices.

Student Guide - page 336 *(Answers on p. 97)*

- Homework is in the *Student Guide.* Students will need *Four-Quadrant Grid Paper.*

- If students do not complete the questions in the *Student Guide* discussion, assign them as homework.

Journal Prompt

Explain why, after completing a slide, the original figure and the image figure are always congruent.

At a Glance

Part 1. Sliding Along

1. Use the *Slides* Activity Pages in the *Discovery Assignment Book* to begin discussion. You may wish to make transparencies of some of the pages. Students complete ***Questions 1–11*** in pairs or in groups.

2. Discuss that a shape moves right 5 units when 5 is added to each *x*-coordinate. ***(Questions 1–2)***

3. Discuss that a shape moves up or forward 5 units when 5 is added to each *y*-coordinate. ***(Questions 3–4)***

4. Explain to students that forward/back movement for Mr. Origin can also be referred to as up/down slides.

5. Discuss right/left and up/down slides in ***Questions 5–11.***

6. Through discussion, help students discover that the figure resulting from a slide is congruent to the original figure.

7. Students complete the Sliding Along section in *These Boots Are Made for Sliding* Activity Pages in the *Student Guide.*

8. Introduce the term image.

9. Discuss corresponding parts of figures and the fact that corresponding sides are parallel.

Part 2. Patterns with Slides

Discuss with the class the patterns in ***Questions 12–15*** and ***Questions 16–19*** in the Patterns with Slides section in the *Student Guide.*

Homework

Assign the homework problems in the *Student Guide.*

Answer Key is on pages 95–99.

Notes:

Name _____ Date _____

_____

Four-column Data Table, Blackline Master

Student Guide (p. 332)

These Boots Are Made for Sliding

1. (3, 2)

2. (-3, 2)

3. Only the *x*-coordinate changed; it is 6 units less.

4. (5, 3)

5. (-1, 3)

6. Only the *x*-coordinate changed, by 6 units less.

7. Only the *x*-coordinate changed. The old *x*-coordinate is (4, 6) while the new is (-2, 6), a difference of 6 units.

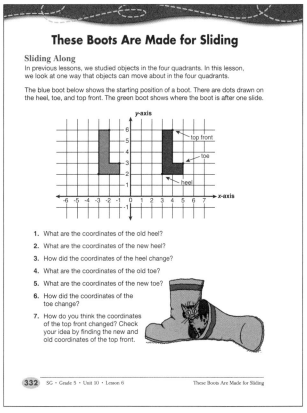

Student Guide - page 332

Student Guide (p. 333)

8. It slid down 2 units and to the right 4 units.

9. The shape slid 4 units to the right; 4 was added to the old *x*-coordinates to get the new *x*-coordinates.

10. The shape slid 2 units down; 2 was subtracted from the old *y*-coordinates to get the new *y*-coordinates.

11. Sides BC and B′C′, Sides AC and A′C′, Vertex B and Vertex B′, Vertex C and Vertex C′

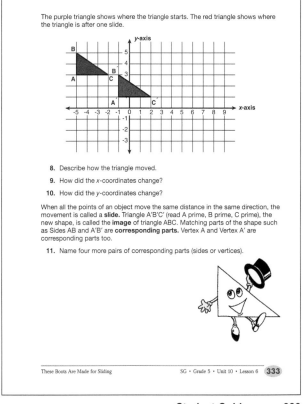

Student Guide - page 333

Student Guide - page 334

Patterns with Slides

The orange boot below shows the starting position. The yellow boot shows where the boot is after one slide. The boot slides again. The red boot shows where the boot is after the second slide.

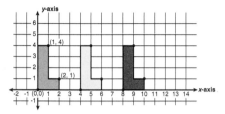

12. Describe how this boot moved.

13. Imagine that the boot follows the same pattern for each slide. Use a *Four-column Data Table* to complete the table.

Slide	Heel Coordinates	Toe Coordinates	Top Front Coordinates
0	(0, 0)	(2, 1)	(1, 4)
1	?	?	(5, 4)
2	?	(10, 1)	?
3	(12, 0)	?	?
4	?	(18, 1)	?
10	?	?	(41, 4)

14. Explain what you did to find the answers in the table.

15. If the heel is at (64, 0), then how many slides has the boot made?

Student Guide - page 334

---

16. In this question, we will study a different boot and a different slide. Use the first row (Slide 0) of the chart to draw the boot on a piece of *Four-Quadrant Grid Paper*. Shade this boot.

Slide	Heel Coordinates	Toe Coordinates	Top Front Coordinates
0	(5, 3)	(7, 4)	(6, 7)
1	(2, 1)	(4, 2)	(3, 5)
2	?	?	?
3	?	?	?
4	?	?	?
5	?	?	?
10	?	?	?

17. Use the second row of the chart in Question 16 to draw the new boot.

18. Fill in the rest of the chart in Question 16.

19. Explain how the boot in Question 16 slides.

Homework

For each shape on the following grid, describe the slide needed to move the purple figure onto its image, the pink figure. How many units to the right or left and up or down is the slide?

1. Parallelogram
2. Triangle
3. Pentagon
4. Rectangle

Student Guide - page 335

Student Guide (p. 334)

12. It slid twice. Both times it slid four units to the right.

13.

Slide	Heel Coordinates	Toe Coordinates	Top Front Coordinates
0	(0, 0)	(2, 1)	(1, 4)
1	(4, 0)	(6, 1)	(5, 4)
2	(8, 0)	(10, 1)	(9, 4)
3	(12, 0)	(14, 1)	(13, 4)
4	(16, 0)	(18, 1)	(17, 4)
5	(20, 0)	(22, 1)	(21, 4)
6	(24, 0)	(26, 1)	(25, 4)
7	(28, 0)	(30, 1)	(29, 4)
8	(32, 0)	(34, 1)	(33, 4)
9	(36, 0)	(38, 1)	(37, 4)
10	(40, 0)	(42, 1)	(41, 4)

14. For each slide, add 4 to each of the heel, toe, and top front *x*-coordinates.

15. 16 slides

Student Guide (p. 335)

16.–17.

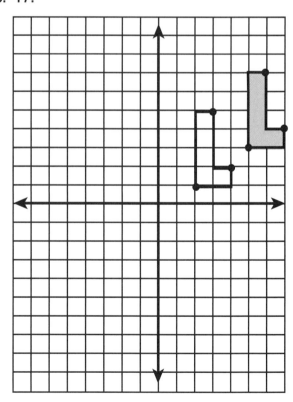

18.

Slide	Heel Coordinates	Toe Coordinates	Top Front Coordinates
0	(5, 3)	(7, 4)	(6, 7)
1	(2, 1)	(4, 2)	(3, 5)
2	(-1, -1)	(1, 0)	(0, 3)
3	(-4, -3)	(-2, -2)	(-3, 1)
4	(-7, -5)	(-5, -4)	(-6, -1)
5	(-10, -7)	(-8, -6)	(-9, -3)
6	(-13, -9)	(-11, -8)	(-12, -5)
7	(-16, -11)	(-14, -10)	(-15, -7)
8	(-19, -13)	(-17, -12)	(-18, -9)
9	(-22, -15)	(-20, -14)	(-21, -11)
10	(-25, -17)	(-23, -16)	(-24, -13)

19. The boot slides to the left 3 units and down 2 units.

Homework

1. 10 units up
2. 10 units to the right and 6 units down
3. 10 units to the left and 2 units up
4. 5 units to the right and 7 units up

Student Guide (p. 336)

5.–7.

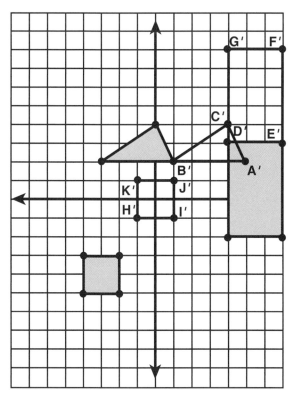

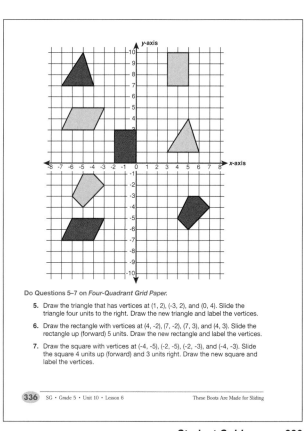

Do Questions 5–7 on *Four-Quadrant Grid Paper*.

5. Draw the triangle that has vertices at (1, 2), (-3, 2), and (0, 4). Slide the triangle four units to the right. Draw the new triangle and label the vertices.

6. Draw the rectangle with vertices at (4, -2), (7, -2), (7, 3), and (4, 3). Slide the rectangle up (forward) 5 units. Draw the new rectangle and label the vertices.

7. Draw the square with vertices at (-4, -5), (-2, -5), (-2, -3), and (-4, -3). Slide the square 4 units up (forward) and 3 units right. Draw the new square and label the vertices.

336 SG • Grade 5 • Unit 10 • Lesson 6   These Boots Are Made for Sliding

Student Guide - page 336

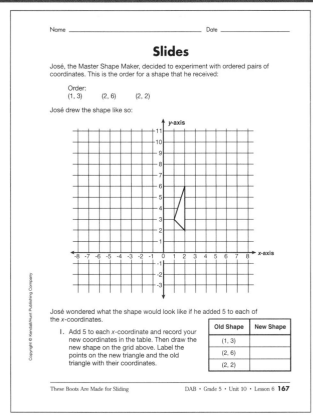

Discovery Assignment Book - page 167

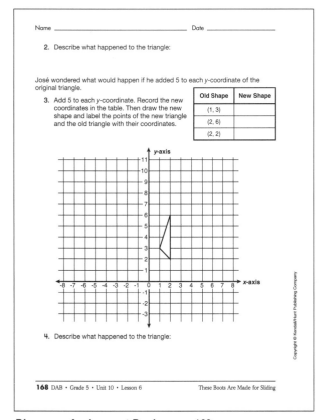

Discovery Assignment Book - page 168

Discovery Assignment Book (pp. 167–168)

Slides

1.*

Old Shape	New Shape
(1, 3)	(1, 8)
(2, 6)	(2, 11)
(2, 2)	(2, 7)

1.–3.

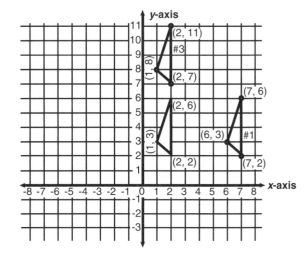

2. The triangle slid 5 units to the right.*

3.*

Old Shape	New Shape
(1, 3)	(1, 8)
(2, 6)	(2, 11)
(2, 2)	(2, 7)

4. The triangle slid 5 units up.*

*Answers and/or discussion are included in the Lesson Guide.

Discovery Assignment Book (p. 169)

5. It slid 4 units to the right.

6.

Boot	Heel Coordinates	Toe Coordinates	Top Front Coordinates
Black Boot	(2,1)	(4, 2)	(3, 5)
White Boot	(6, 1)	(8, 2)	(7, 5)

7. *x*-coordinate

8. *y*-coordinate

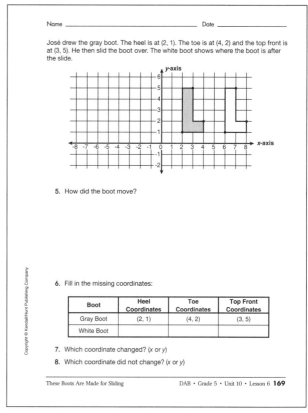

Name _____ Date _____

José drew the gray boot. The heel is at (2, 1). The toe is at (4, 2) and the top front is at (3, 5). He then slid the boot over. The white boot shows where the boot is after the slide.

5. How did the boot move?

6. Fill in the missing coordinates:

Boot	Heel Coordinates	Toe Coordinates	Top Front Coordinates
Gray Boot	(2, 1)	(4, 2)	(3, 5)
White Boot			

7. Which coordinate changed? (*x* or *y*)

8. Which coordinate did not change? (*x* or *y*)

These Boots Are Made for Sliding   DAB • Grade 5 • Unit 10 • Lesson 6 **169**

Discovery Assignment Book - page 169

Discovery Assignment Book (p. 171)

9.

Boot	Heel Coordinates	Toe Coordinates	Top Front Coordinates
Black Boot	(-6,-5)	(-4, -4)	(-5, -1)
White Boot	(-6, 4)	(-4, 5)	(-5, 8)

The *x*-coordinates stayed the same. The boot slid 9 units up so 9 was added to each of the *y*-coordinates.

10.

Triangle	Vertex A Coordinates	Vertex B Coordinates	Vertex C Coordinates
Black Triangle	(1, 8)	(2, 10)	(3, 8)
White Triangle	(5, 3)	(6, 5)	(7, 3)

The *x*- and *y*-coordinates changed. The triangle slid 4 units to the right and 5 units down; 4 was added to each *x*-coordinate; 5 was subtracted from each *y*-coordinate.

11.

Square	Vertex R Coordinates	Vertex S Coordinates	Vertex T Coordinates	Vertex U Coordinates
Black Square	(1, -3)	(3, -3)	(3, -1)	(1, -1)
White Square	(-3, 1)	(-1, 1)	(-1, 3)	(-3, 3)

The *x*- and *y*-coordinates changed. The square slid 4 units up and 4 units to the left; 4 was subtracted from each *x*-coordinate and 4 was added to each *y*-coordinate.

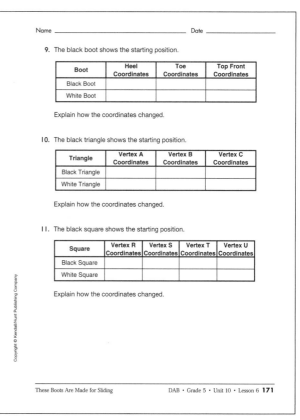

Name _____ Date _____

9. The black boot shows the starting position.

Boot	Heel Coordinates	Toe Coordinates	Top Front Coordinates
Black Boot			
White Boot			

Explain how the coordinates changed.

10. The black triangle shows the starting position.

Triangle	Vertex A Coordinates	Vertex B Coordinates	Vertex C Coordinates
Black Triangle			
White Triangle			

Explain how the coordinates changed.

11. The black square shows the starting position.

Square	Vertex R Coordinates	Vertex S Coordinates	Vertex T Coordinates	Vertex U Coordinates
Black Square				
White Square				

Explain how the coordinates changed.

These Boots Are Made for Sliding   DAB • Grade 5 • Unit 10 • Lesson 6 **171**

Discovery Assignment Book - page 171

These Boots Are Made for Flipping

Lesson Overview

Students investigate flips. They find that flipping a shape over the y-axis changes the sign of the x-coordinate while flipping over the x-axis changes the sign of the y-coordinate.

Key Content

- Using flips to move shapes about the coordinate system.
- Determining the image of a flip.

Key Vocabulary

- flip
- line of reflection

Homework

Assign the Homework section in the *Student Guide.*

Assessment

Use the *Moving Shapes* Assessment Pages as a quiz.

Students studied line symmetry in Grades 1 through 3 and in Unit 9 Lesson 3 of fourth grade.

Materials List

Supplies and Copies

Student	Teacher
Supplies for Each Student Pair	**Supplies**
• scissors	
Copies	**Copies/Transparencies**
• 1 copy of *Moving Shapes* per student (*Unit Resource Guide* Pages 108–109)	• 1 transparency of *Flips*, optional (*Discovery Assignment Book* Pages 173–174)
• several copies of *Four-Quadrant Grid Paper* per student (*Unit Resource Guide* Page 47)	• 1 transparency of *Four-Quadrant Grid Paper* (*Unit Resource Guide* Page 47)
• 1 copy of *Centimeter Graph Paper* per student (*Unit Resource Guide* Page 110)	

All blackline masters including assessment, transparency, and DPP masters are also on the Teacher Resource CD.

Student Books

These Boots Are Made for Flipping (*Student Guide* Pages 337–342)
Flips (*Discovery Assignment Book* Pages 173–174)

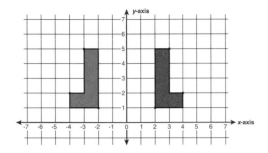

These Boots Are Made for Flipping

1. Trace and cut out a boot from graph paper that is like the blue boot. Shade in the boot and place it on top of the blue boot here.
2. Can you slide your boot, without lifting the boot off the paper, onto the green boot? Why or why not?

To move the blue boot onto the green boot in one move, we have to **flip** the blue boot over a line. That line is called the **line of reflection.**

3. Where is the line of reflection in the picture?

4. Make a table like the one below and complete it.

Boot	Heel Coordinates	Toe Coordinates	Top Front Coordinates
Blue Boot	?	?	?
Green Boot	?	?	?

5. Explain how the x-coordinates changed in Question 4.

6. Explain how the y-coordinates changed in Question 4.

These Boots Are Made for Flipping SG • Grade 5 • Unit 10 • Lesson 7 **337**

Student Guide - page 337 *(Answers on p. 111)*

(Answers on p. 111)

TIMS Tip

Note to students that the word flip is used precisely. No other motion, such as a slide or a turn, is allowed in a flip.

Teaching the Activity

In this activity, only flips over the x-axis and y-axis will be discussed.

Ask students to open to the *These Boots Are Made for Flipping* Activity Pages in the *Student Guide.* Distribute *Centimeter Graph Paper* to each student. A quarter sheet is enough for students to trace and cut out a blue boot like the one shown *(Question 1).* Draw the boots shown in *Question 1* on a transparency of *Four-Quadrant Grid Paper.* Use a cut-out boot on the transparency as well. Discuss *Question 2* with students. Allow them time to discover that it is impossible to slide the blue boot onto the green boot. To move the blue boot onto the green boot, a **flip** is needed. Another name for a flip is a reflection. Note to students that the shape resulting from a flip is called the **image,** just as the result of a slide is called an image of the original figure. The image of a flip is a reflection in the line of reflection.

Content Note

Line of Reflection. Show students that when a figure is flipped over the **line of reflection,** the two parts match exactly. Corresponding points are equidistant from the line of reflection. Two examples are shown in Figure 13. The line of reflection for the quadrilaterals is the y-axis while the line of reflection for the triangles is the x-axis.

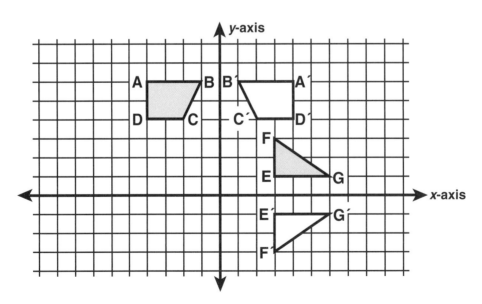

Figure 13: *Examples of flips: quadrilateral ABCD is flipped over the y-axis; triangle EFG over the x-axis.*

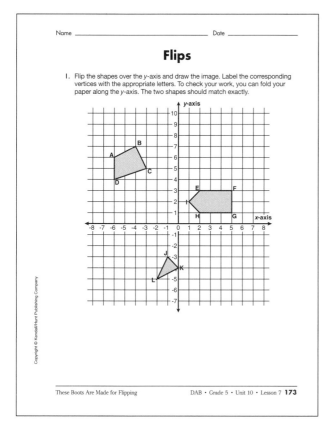

Discovery Assignment Book - page 173 *(Answers on p. 113)*

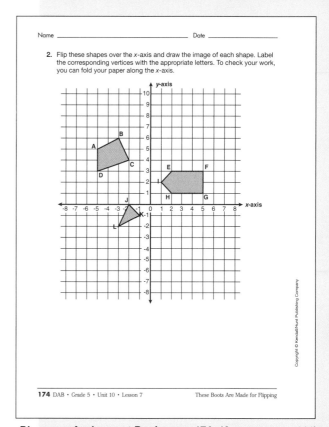

Discovery Assignment Book - page 174 *(Answers on p. 114)*

Students should complete the *Flips* Activity Pages in the *Discovery Assignment Book* at this time. These problems provide practice in finding and drawing the images of flips over the *x* and *y* axes. Note to students that corresponding vertices are the same distance from the line of reflection. For example, in ***Question 1,*** vertex B is 4 units from the *y*-axis (the line of reflection). Therefore, vertex B′ must be 4 units from the *y*-axis. This is illustrated in Figure 14.

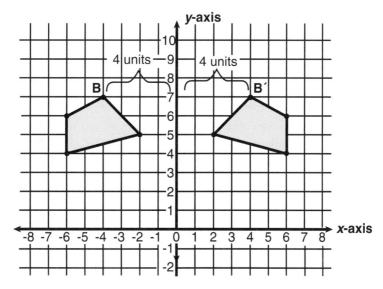

Figure 14: *Corresponding vertices are the same distance from the line of reflection.*

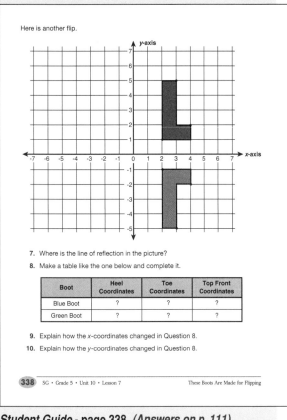

Here is another flip.

7. Where is the line of reflection in the picture?

8. Make a table like the one below and complete it.

Boot	Heel Coordinates	Toe Coordinates	Top Front Coordinates
Blue Boot	?	?	?
Green Boot	?	?	?

9. Explain how the x-coordinates changed in Question 8.

10. Explain how the y-coordinates changed in Question 8.

Student Guide - page 338 *(Answers on p. 111)*

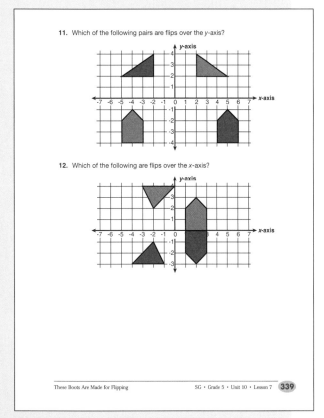

11. Which of the following pairs are flips over the y-axis?

12. Which of the following are flips over the x-axis?

Student Guide - page 339 *(Answers on p. 112)*

After they complete the *Flips* Activity Pages in the *Discovery Assignment Book,* ask students to continue the *These Boots Are Made for Flipping* Activity Pages in the *Student Guide.* **Question 4** asks students to find the coordinates of a boot and its image. To answer **Questions 5–6,** children should notice in their chart that the *x*-coordinates have the same value, but now have opposite signs. The *y*-coordinates remain unchanged.

Ask children to complete **Questions 7–10** individually or in groups and discuss the results together. They should conclude that the boot flipped over the *x*-axis, so the *x*-axis is the line of reflection. In this figure, the *x*-coordinates remained unchanged, but the *y*-coordinates changed signs.

Content Note

Make sure students understand that to do a flip, the line of reflection must be specified. To do a slide, the direction(s) and the number of units must be given.

Questions 11–12 ask students to identify flips. In **Question 11,** the triangle is flipped over the *y*-axis, but the pentagon is not. In **Question 12,** the pentagon is a flip over the *x*-axis, but the triangle is not.

Questions 13–15 help children generalize further to see what happens to the coordinates when figures are flipped over the *x*- and the *y*-axis.

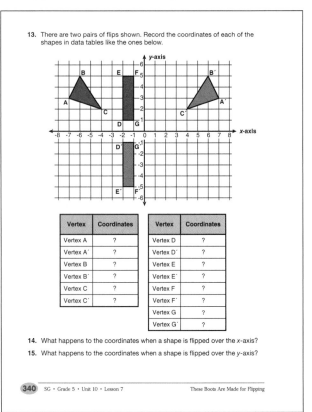

13. There are two pairs of flips shown. Record the coordinates of each of the shapes in data tables like the ones below.

Vertex	Coordinates
Vertex A	?
Vertex A´	?
Vertex B	?
Vertex B´	?
Vertex C	?
Vertex C´	?

Vertex	Coordinates
Vertex D	?
Vertex D´	?
Vertex E	?
Vertex E´	?
Vertex F	?
Vertex F´	?
Vertex G	?
Vertex G´	?

14. What happens to the coordinates when a shape is flipped over the x-axis?

15. What happens to the coordinates when a shape is flipped over the y-axis?

Student Guide - page 340 *(Answers on p. 112)*

Homework and Practice

Assign the Homework section in the *Student Guide*.

Journal Prompt

Write a letter to a friend explaining the difference between a slide and a flip.

Assessment

Use the *Moving Shapes* Assessment Pages in the *Unit Resource Guide*. It is easier for children if the two pages are copied on separate sheets of paper. Students will also need two sheets of *Four-Quadrant Grid Paper*.

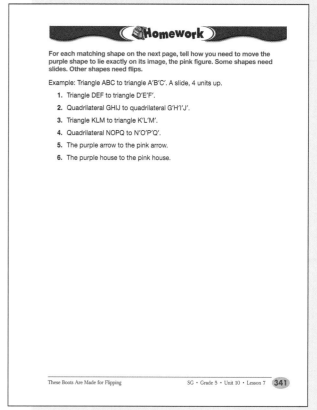

Student Guide - page 341 (Answers on p. 113)

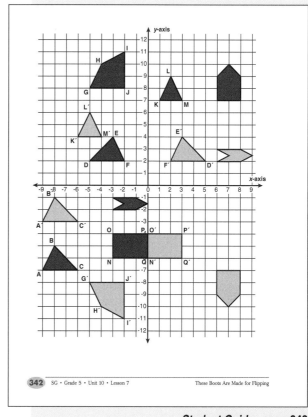

Student Guide - page 342

Another type of transformation besides flips and slides are enlargements. Introduce enlargements by asking students to place a boot in the first quadrant of a piece of *Four-Quadrant Grid Paper,* with the heel at (0, 0) as shown in Figure 15. Have them record the coordinates of the heel, toe, and top front of the boot in this first column of a data table. In an adjacent column, have them multiply each coordinate by 2 and then plot the new boot as shown in Figure 15. Discuss with the class that the new figure is the same shape as the old, just larger. Remind students that these are similar shapes. You may also wish to discuss enlargements of photographs. To challenge students, ask them how the area of the figure changes after an enlargement. Ask:

*   *What happens if all the coordinates are multiplied by 3?*

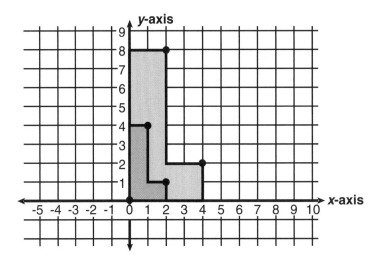

	Blue Boot	Green Boot
Heel	(0, 0)	(0, 0)
Toe	(2, 1)	(4, 2)
Top Right	(1, 4)	(2, 8)

Figure 15: *Enlarging a boot*

At a Glance

Teaching the Activity

1. Discuss *Questions 1–3* on *These Boots Are Made for Flipping* Activity Pages in the *Student Guide* using the overhead projector.
2. Explain that flips are reflections about a line of reflection.
3. Students complete the *Flips* Activity Pages in the *Discovery Assignment Book* in groups or individually.
4. Continue discussing *These Boots Are Made for Flipping* Activity Pages in the *Student Guide.* Students complete *Questions 4–13.*
5. Conclude that flips over the *y*-axis cause the *x*-coordinates to change signs, while flips over the *y*-axis change the sign of the *x*-coordinates *(Questions 14–15).*

Homework

Assign the Homework section in the *Student Guide.*

Assessment

Use the *Moving Shapes* Assessment Pages as a quiz.

Extension

Introduce students to enlargements using the boot shape and a piece of *Four-Quadrant Grid Paper.*

Answer Key is on pages 111–114.

Notes:

Moving Shapes

Tell how to move the shaded shape onto the white shape. For flips, give the line of reflection. For slides, give the direction(s) and the number of units. You will need two sheets of *Four-Quadrant Grid Paper.*

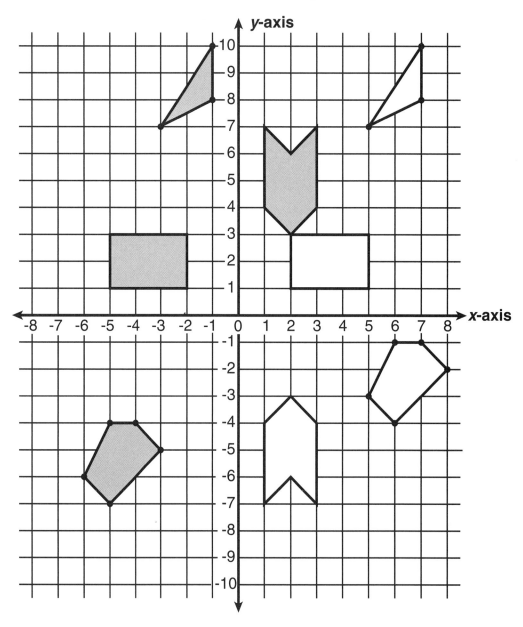

Assessment Blackline Master

Name _____   Date _____

1. Triangle

2. Arrow

3. Rectangle

4. Pentagon

5. On a new sheet of grid paper, graph the ordered pairs: (-2, 3), (0, 1), (2, 2), (1, 5). Connect the points in order using line segments.

6. Slide the shape 4 units up and left 5 units. Draw the image and shade it in.

7. Flip the original shape in Question 5 over the x-axis. Draw the shape and label the new coordinates.

Name _____ Date _____

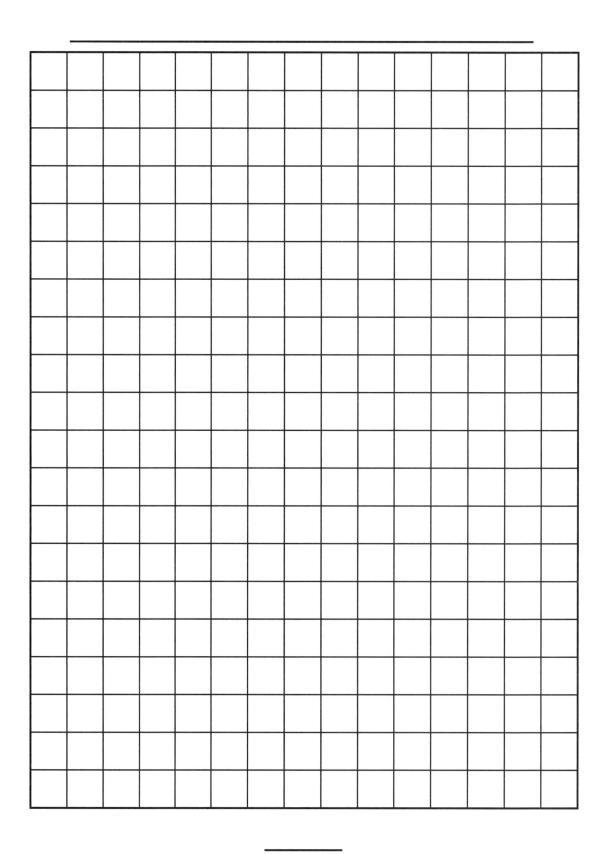

Centimeter Graph Paper, Assessment Blackline Master

Student Guide (p. 337)

These Boots Are Made for Flipping

1. Students replicate the figure in the *Student Guide*.*

2. No*

3. The *y*-axis is the line of reflection.

4.

Boot	Heel Coordinates	Toe Coordinates	Top Front Coordinates
Blue Boot	(2, 1)	(4, 2)	(3, 5)
Green Boot	(-2, 1)	(-4, 2)	(-3, 5)

5. The *x*-coordinates have the same number but now have opposite signs.*

6. The *y*-coordinates remain unchanged.*

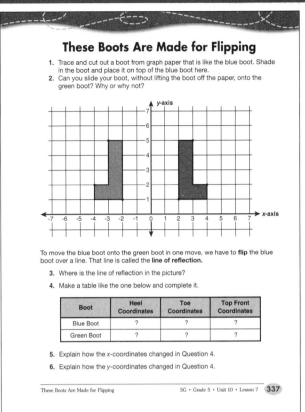

Student Guide - page 337

Student Guide (p. 338)

7. The *x*-axis is the line of reflection.

8.

Boot	Heel Coordinates	Toe Coordinates	Top Front Coordinates
Blue Boot	(2, 1)	(4, 2)	(3, 5)
Green Boot	(2, -1)	(4, -2)	(3, -5)

9. The *x*-coordinates remain unchanged.

10. The *y*-coordinates have the same number but now have opposite signs.

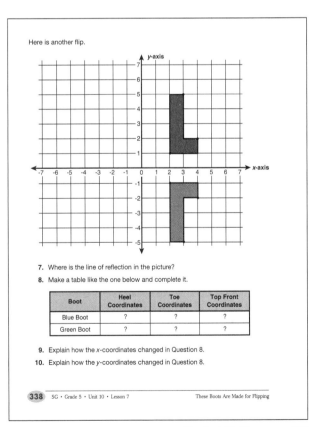

Student Guide - page 338

*Answers and/or discussion are included in the Lesson Guide.

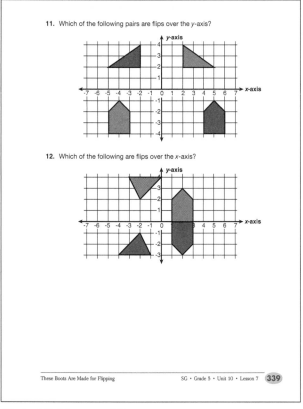

Student Guide - page 339

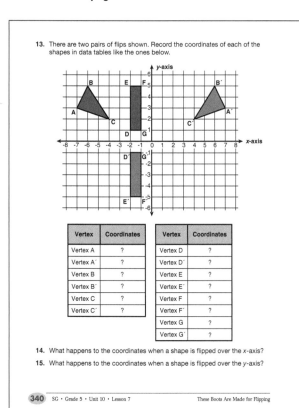

Student Guide - page 340

Student Guide (p. 339)

11. The triangles show flips over the *y*-axis. (Since the distance of the blue pentagon from the *y*-axis is not the same as the distance of the green pentagon from the *y*-axis, the pentagons do not show a flip.)

12. The pentagons show flips over the *x*-axis. (The blue triangle is not flipped over the axis since its distance from the *x*-axis is not the same as the distance of the green triangle from the *x*-axis. Also, in order to place the triangle onto its image a rotation would have to take place.)

Student Guide (p. 340)

13.

Vertex	Coordinates
Vertex A	(-7, 3)
Vertex A´	(7, 3)
Vertex B	(-6, 5)
Vertex B´	(6, 5)
Vertex C	(-4, 2)
Vertex C´	(4, 2)

Vertex	Coordinates
Vertex D	(-2, 1)
Vertex D´	(-2, -1)
Vertex E	(-2, 5)
Vertex E´	(-2, -5)
Vertex F	(-1, 5)
Vertex F´	(-1, -5)
Vertex G	(-1, 1)
Vertex G´	(-1, -1)

14. The *x*-coordinates remain unchanged. The *y*-coordinates have the same number but opposite signs.

15. The *y*-coordinates remain unchanged. The *x*-coordinates have the same number but opposite signs.

Student Guide (p. 341)

Homework

1. A flip over the *y*-axis.

2. A flip over the *x*-axis.

3. A slide 3 units down and 7 units to the left.

4. A slide 3 units to the right.

5. A slide 9 units to the right and 4 units up.

6. A flip over the *x*-axis.

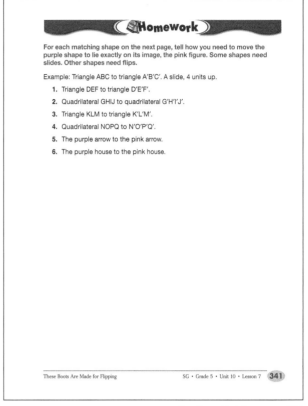

Student Guide - page 341

Discovery Assignment Book (p. 173)

Flips

1.

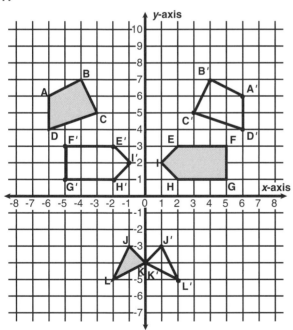

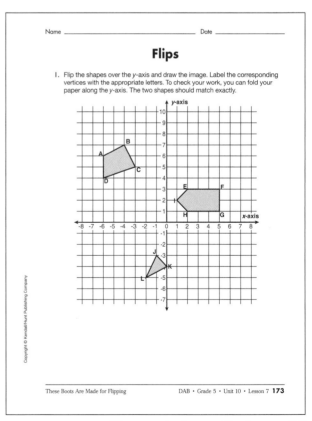

Discovery Assignment Book - page 173

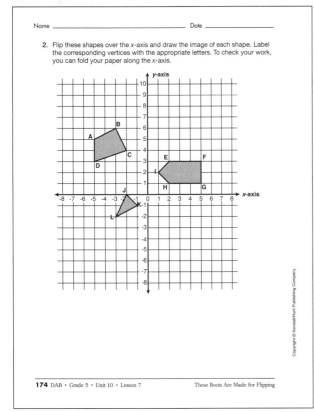

Discovery Assignment Book - page 174

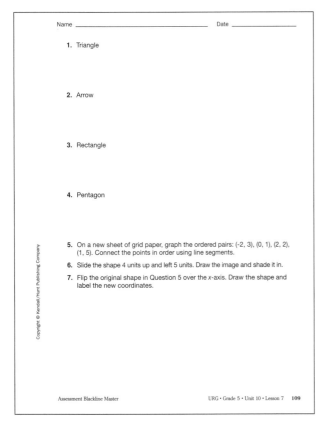

Unit Resource Guide - page 109

Discovery Assignment Book (p. 174)

2.

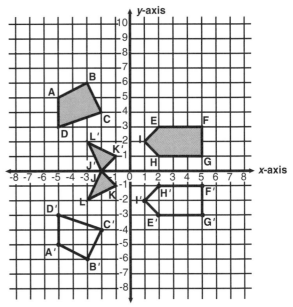

Unit Resource Guide (p. 109)

Moving Shapes

1. A slide 8 units to the right.

2. A flip over the x-axis.

3. A flip over the y-axis or a slide 7 units right.

4. A slide 11 units to the right and 3 units up.

5.–7.

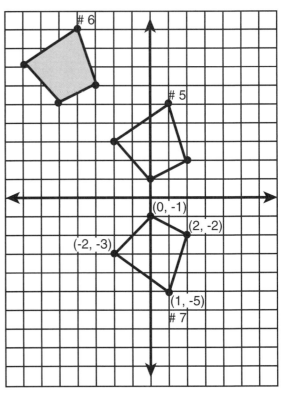

Reading a Map

Lesson Overview

Map reading is one of the most common uses of a coordinate system in everyday life. In this lesson, students read maps for both specific locations and to find distances.

Key Content

• Using a coordinate system to find locations on a map.
• Using the scale on a map.

Math Facts

DPP item O reviews math facts.

Homework

1. Assign the Homework section on the *Reading a Map* Activity Pages in the *Student Guide.*
2. Assign Part 6 of the Home Practice.

Assessment

Use the *Carol's Chicago Map* Assessment Pages as an assessment.

Curriculum Sequence

After This Unit

Using a map scale is a type of proportional reasoning. Proportional reasoning is explored in greater depth in Unit 13.

Materials List

Supplies and Copies

Student	Teacher
Supplies for Each Student	**Supplies**
Copies	**Copies/Transparencies**
• 1 copy of *Carol's Chicago Map* per student (*Unit Resource Guide* Pages 121–122)	• 1 transparency of *Chicago Grid* (*Unit Resource Guide* Page 123) • 1 transparency of *Chicago Map* (*Unit Resource Guide* Page 124) • 1 copy of *TIMS Multidimensional Rubric* (*Teacher Implementation Guide*, Assessment section)

All blackline masters including assessment, transparency, and DPP masters are also on the Teacher Resource CD.

Student Books
Reading a Map (*Student Guide* Pages 343–344)
Student Rubric: *Knowing* (*Student Guide* Appendix A and Inside Back Cover)

Daily Practice and Problems and Home Practice
DPP items O–P (*Unit Resource Guide* Pages 20–21)
Home Practice Part 6 (*Discovery Assignment Book* Page 164)

Note: Classrooms whose pacing differs significantly from the suggested pacing of the units should use the Math Facts Calendar in Section 4 of the *Facts Resource Guide* to ensure students receive the complete math facts program.

Assessment Tools
TIMS Multidimensional Rubric (*Teacher Implementation Guide*, Assessment section)

O. Bit: Practice: 2s and Squares
(URG p. 20)

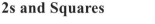

A. $10 \div 5 =$ B. $25 \div 5 =$

C. $20 \div 2 =$ D. $6 \div 3 =$

E. $4 \div 2 =$ F. $9 \div 3 =$

G. $36 \div 6 =$ H. $8 \div 2 =$

I. $100 \div 10 =$ J. $12 \div 2 =$

K. $64 \div 8 =$ L. $14 \div 7 =$

M. $16 \div 2 =$ N. $49 \div 7 =$

O. $16 \div 4 =$ P. $18 \div 9 =$

Q. $81 \div 9 =$

P. Challenge: Slow and Steady (URG p. 21)

Four children race their pet turtles. The turtles are named Tee Tee, Truth, Pokey, and Speedy. They used their pets' favorite foods (strawberries, lettuce, cantaloupe, and beets) to get them to cross the finish line. Read these clues to find which food each turtle likes best and in what order they finished the race.

Clues:

A. Truth finished before the turtle who loves lettuce and the turtle who craves cantaloupe, but after Tee Tee.

B. Pokey finished after the turtle who loves strawberries and the turtle with a taste for beets, but before the turtle who prefers cantaloupe.

C. Truth does not like strawberries.

Reading a Map

Suzanne is a big fan of Carlton Fisk, the great catcher who played with both the Boston Red Sox and the Chicago White Sox. When she traveled with her family, she looked for places that might have "Fisk" in the name. One summer, her family was planning a trip to Alabama. She looked in an atlas at a list of the names of towns and found that there was indeed a Fisk, Alabama. Next, she looked at a map.

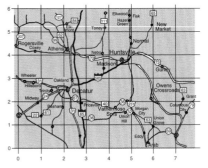

Suzanne had a very difficult time locating Fisk. If you were with her, how might you help her? What do you know about the way maps and atlases work that would aid in finding Fisk?

Suzanne's mother pointed out that it is possible to use the numbers on the map in the same way Suzanne had used a coordinate system in school. When Suzanne looked up Fisk again in the atlas, she paid attention to the ordered pairs following the name. She found (5, 6). Suzanne also learned that a lot of maps use a combination of letters and numbers as a coordinate system. On another map, for example, Fisk might be named as (E, 6).

Reading a Map   SG • Grade 5 • Unit 10 • Lesson 8   **343**

Student Guide - page 343

---

1. Use this information to find Fisk on the map. Is Fisk at exactly (5, 6)? What are the coordinates designed to do?

Use the map to answer the following questions.

2. What town is located at about (3, 2)?

3. Look at the four ordered pairs (1, 2), (1, 3), (2, 2), and (2, 3). What town is located almost in the center of all the points?

Homework

Using a Map to Find Distances

The map of north central Alabama on the previous page has a scale in which 1 centimeter represents 10 miles. Use the ordered pairs below to help you locate the towns and solve the distance problems. You will need your ruler. Measure distances "as the crow flies."

Athens (2, 4)	Elkmont (2, 5)	Grant (7, 2)
New Market (6, 5)	Owens Crossroads (6, 2)	Priceville (3, 2)
Toney (4, 5)	Union Grove (6, 1)	Morgan City (5, 1)

1. About how far is it from Morgan City to Grant?

2. About how far is it from Union Grove to Toney?

3. About how far is it from Priceville to New Market?

4. Suppose you traveled from Grant to New Market to Elkmont. How many miles would you have gone?

5. If you wanted to travel to all the towns listed above without zig-zagging across the region, in what order might you travel? How many miles would you cover? Think about the shortest route possible. Plan to share your proposed route with the class.

344 SG • Grade 5 • Unit 10 • Lesson 8   Reading a Map

Student Guide - page 344 (Answers on p. 125)

Teaching the Activity

Part 1 Introducing Chicago

The *Reading a Map* Activity Pages in the *Student Guide* highlight the use of ordered pairs in the context of a map. Note to students that highway maps often number or letter the spaces, not the lines. (Scientists and mathematicians number the lines because it is a more precise way to specify locations.) Discuss **Question 1,** then have students work through **Questions 2–3.**

After the questions, place a *Chicago Map* Transparency on the overhead. All the addresses in Chicago are given in relation to the corner of State Street and Madison Street, with that corner considered the point of origin.

Content Note

Not Quite Chicago. The map on the transparency is not an exact map of Chicago's downtown area. Not all the streets are represented. Because city blocks can vary in length, the distances students are asked to calculate should be viewed as approximations.

Show students the corner of State Street and Madison Street. They should realize that a grid can be placed over this map. Place a transparency of the *Chicago Grid* over the *Chicago Map.*

With the grid overlay in place, pose the following questions:

- *What is located near (-6, 1)?* (Opera House)
- *What building is located between (-4, 6) and (-6, 6)?* (Merchandise Mart)

Introduce the idea of using the grid to measure distances between points on the map. Sometimes we want to know how far it is from one location to another, traveling on the streets. Other times we measure distances "as the crow flies."

Ask a student to find the distance between the Sears Tower and the Opera House. An "E" is used to show the entrances to the buildings. Distances are measured from entrance to entrance. Since on the map 1 cm represents $\frac{1}{8}$ mile, that distance is about $\frac{3}{8}$ mile, straight up Wacker Drive. Ask:

- *How far is the walk between the Federal Building and the Prudential Building if you walk along the streets?* (about 10 cm or $1\frac{1}{4}$ miles)
- *How far is the Federal Building from the Prudential Building "as the crow flies"?* (between 7 cm and 8 cm or a little less than one mile.)

Pose the problem:

- *Sam is standing at the corner of Dearborn and Van Buren. He needs to go to the Prudential Building. In what directions and how far does he need to walk?* (Sam needs to walk north for $\frac{7}{8}$ mile and then walk east for a little more than $\frac{3}{8}$ mile.)

Part 2 *Carol's Chicago Map* **Assessment**

Use the *Carol's Chicago Map* Assessment Pages in the *Unit Resource Guide* as an assessment. (*Carol's Chicago Map* is not a precise map of Chicago.) Remind students of the guidelines they should follow when using the *Knowing* Student Rubric.

The questions show whether students understand both the coordinate system and how to calculate distances when a scale is used. Also, fractions are used in a map-reading context. Look to see whether students correctly use eighths and whether they use mixed numbers when reporting distances.

Math Facts

DPP item O reviews the division facts for the 2s and the square numbers.

Homework and Practice

- Assign the Homework section on the *Reading a Map* Activity Pages in the *Student Guide*.
- Assign Part 6 of the Home Practice, which is a set of word problems.

Answers for Part 6 of the Home Practice are in the Answer Key at the end of this lesson and at the end of this unit.

Assessment

Use the *Carol's Chicago Map* Assessment Pages to assess students' understanding of the coordinate system. Remind students to measure walking distances along the streets and not "as the crow flies." Note: The map is on centimeter grid paper. Have students focus on the *Knowing* Student Rubric as they complete the assessment. Use the Knowing dimension of the *TIMS Multidimensional Rubric* to score their work on this assessment.

Extension

- Use a local map to find distances between places in the neighborhood. Real estate agents are often a good source for local maps.
- Assign DPP Challenge P.

Name _____ Date _____

PART 6 Sunny Vacation

Choose an appropriate method to solve each of the following problems. For some questions you may need to find an exact answer, while for others you may only need an estimate. For each question, you may choose to use paper and pencil, mental math, or a calculator. Use a separate sheet of paper to explain how you solved each problem.

1. Brett and Reggie plan to fly away to Faraway Island. The Get-Up-And-Go Travel Agency has a sale in progress. If you buy one round trip ticket for $899.99, you will get a second ticket free. Global Travel is offering round trip tickets to Faraway Island for $452.99. Which travel agency offers the best deal for Brett and Reggie? Why?

2. Joanne is going to Faraway Island by herself for seven days. She has $2000 to spend. If she buys one airline ticket from Global Travel, about how much money can she spend each day?

3. Nicole won a free airline ticket to Faraway Island. She has $1000 to spend while she is there.
   A. Nicole plans to spend $\frac{1}{2}$ of the money on hotel accommodations. It costs $79 per night to stay at the Sunset Beach Lodge. Is it within Nicole's budget to stay at the lodge for 6 nights?
   B. If Nicole plans to spend $\frac{1}{2}$ of the money on hotel accommodations and $\frac{1}{4}$ of it on food, about how much money will she have left to spend on souvenirs and entertainment?

4. Lucky Louise went bargain hunting. She found a fan for $0.65, 7 matching pens for $0.15 apiece, and a special on pencils—5 for $1.60. If she buys 2 fans, all 7 matching pens, and only 3 pencils, how much money will she spend?

5. As Brett and Reggie board the plane to return home, the temperature on Faraway Island is 90°F. Brett must return to Minneapolis where it is -10°F. Reggie must return to Milwaukee where it is -7°F.
   A. Where is it colder, Minneapolis or Milwaukee? How much colder?
   B. What is the difference in temperature between Minneapolis and Faraway Island?

164 DAB · Grade 5 · Unit 10   MAPS AND COORDINATES

Discovery Assignment Book - page 164 (Answers on p. 125)

Math Facts and Daily Practice and Problems

Assign DPP items O and P. Item O reviews math facts. DPP item P is a challenging logic problem.

Part 1. Introducing Chicago

1. Use the *Reading a Map* Activity Pages in the *Student Guide* to introduce map coordinates as ordered pairs. *(Questions 1–3)*
2. Use the *Chicago Map* and the *Chicago Grid* Transparency Masters to introduce four-quadrant maps.

Part 2. *Carol's Chicago Map* Assessment

Review the *Knowing* Student Rubric.

Homework

1. Assign the Homework section on the *Reading a Map* Activity Pages in the *Student Guide.*
2. Assign Part 6 of the Home Practice.

Assessment

Use the *Carol's Chicago Map* Assessment Pages as an assessment.

Extension

1. Use a local map to find distances between places in a neighborhood.
2. Assign DPP Challenge P.

Answer Key is on pages 125–126.

Notes:

Carol's Chicago Map

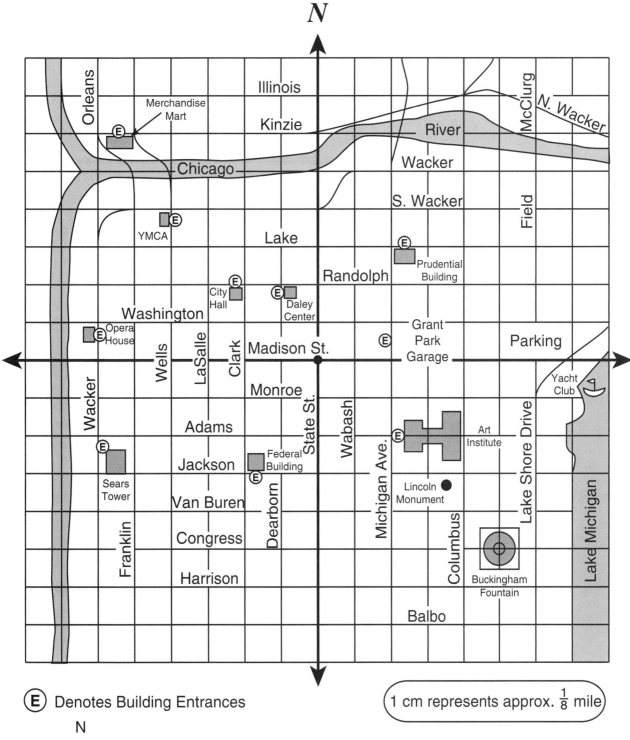

Ⓔ Denotes Building Entrances

1 cm represents approx. $\frac{1}{8}$ mile

Name _____   Date _____

Use the map to answer the following questions. The origin of the map is at the corner of State Street and Madison Street. Measure distances from the entrance to each location. The entrance is marked with an Ⓔ. Measure all walking distances along streets.

1. If you walk from the Sears Tower to Buckingham Fountain, about how far would you walk?

2. If you walk from (-6, -3) to (-1, -3) to (0, 0), about how far would you walk?

3. If you park in the Grant Park Garage and then go to the Opera House, about how far would you walk?

4. If you were at (1, -7), about how far would you walk to get to the Merchandise Mart?

Chicago Grid

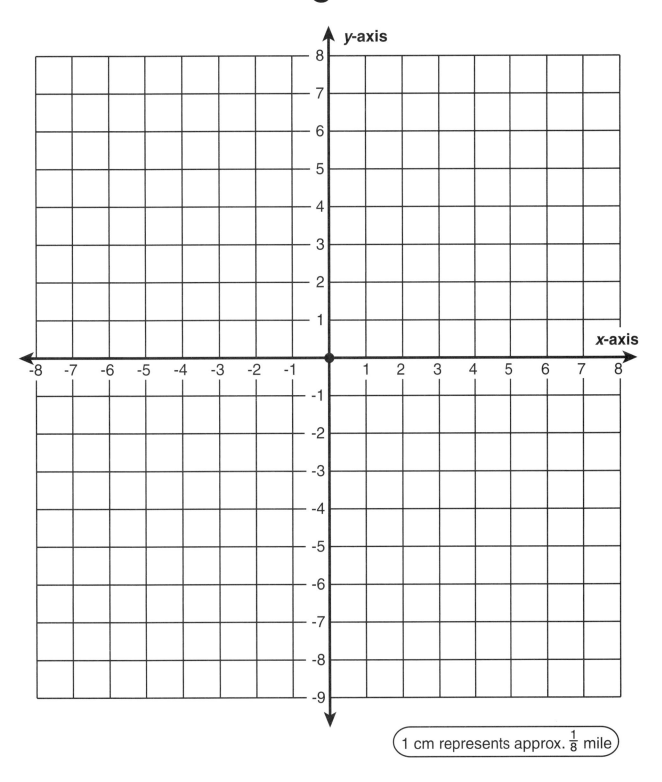

1 cm represents approx. $\frac{1}{8}$ mile

Chicago Map

N

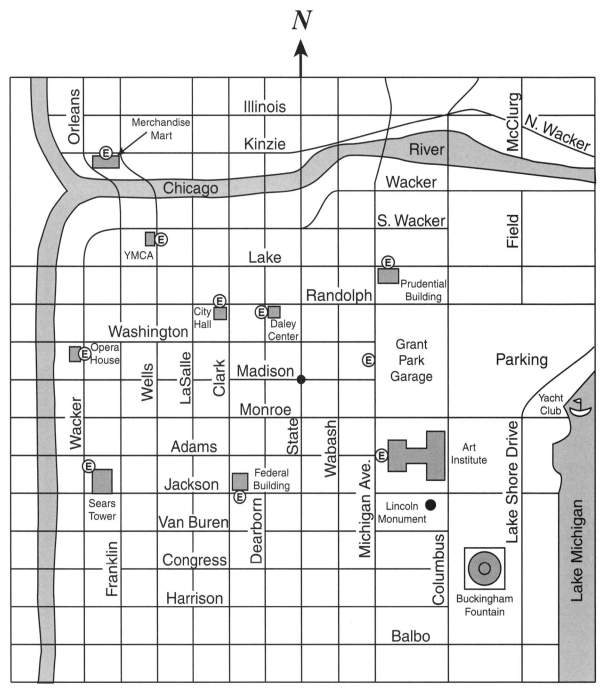

(E) Denotes Building Entrances

1 cm represents approx. $\frac{1}{8}$ mile

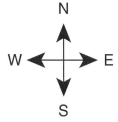

Student Guide (p. 344)

1. No. Coordinates describe the approximate location; (5, 6) is close to Fisk.

2. Priceville

3. Trinity

Homework

1. About 35–40 miles

2. About 75 miles

3. About 70–75 miles

4. About 115 miles

5. Athens to Elkmont, to Toney to New Market, to Owens Crossroads to Grant, to Union Grove to Morgan City, to Priceville. About 240 miles.

1. Use this information to find Fisk on the map. Is Fisk at exactly (5, 6)? What are the coordinates designed to do?

Use the map to answer the following questions.

2. What town is located at about (3, 2)?

3. Look at the four ordered pairs (1, 2), (1, 3), (2, 2), and (2, 3). What town is located almost in the center of all the points?

Homework

Using a Map to Find Distances

The map of north central Alabama on the previous page has a scale in which 1 centimeter represents 10 miles. Use the ordered pairs below to help you locate the towns and solve the distance problems. You will need your ruler. Measure distances "as the crow flies."

Athens (2, 4)	Elkmont (2, 5)	Grant (7, 2)
New Market (6, 5)	Owens Crossroads (6, 2)	Priceville (3, 2)
Toney (4, 5)	Union Grove (6, 1)	Morgan City (5, 1)

1. About how far is it from Morgan City to Grant?

2. About how far is it from Union Grove to Toney?

3. About how far is it from Priceville to New Market?

4. Suppose you traveled from Grant to New Market to Elkmont. How many miles would you have gone?

5. If you wanted to travel to all the towns listed above without zig-zagging across the region, in what order might you travel? How many miles would you cover? Think about the shortest route possible. Plan to share your proposed route with the class.

344   SG • Grade 5 • Unit 10 • Lesson 8   Reading a Map

Student Guide - page 344

Discovery Assignment Book (p. 164)

Home Practice*

Part 6. Sunny Vacation

1. Get-Up-And-Go Travel Agency; 452.99×2 is over $900.

2. Estimates will vary. She will have $1547.01 to spend; $1547.01 \div 7$ is about $200 a day.

3. **A.** Yes. She wants to spend $500 on hotel accommodations; 79×5 is about $400.

    B. $250

4. $3.31

5. **A.** Minneapolis; 3 degrees colder

    B. 100 degrees

Name _____ Date _____

PART 6 Sunny Vacation

Choose an appropriate method to solve each of the following problems. For some questions you may need to find an exact answer, while for others you may only need an estimate. For each question, you may choose to use paper and pencil, mental math, or a calculator. Use a separate sheet of paper to explain how you solved each problem.

1. Brett and Reggie plan to fly away to Faraway Island. The Get-Up-And-Go Travel Agency has a sale in progress. If you buy one round trip ticket for $899.99, you will get a second ticket free. Global Travel is offering round trip tickets to Faraway Island for $452.99. Which travel agency offers the best deal for Brett and Reggie? Why?

2. Joanne is going to Faraway Island by herself for seven days. She has $2000 to spend. If she buys one airline ticket from Global Travel, about how much money can she spend each day?

3. Nicole won a free airline ticket to Faraway Island. She has $1000 to spend while she is there.

   A. Nicole plans to spend $\frac{1}{2}$ of the money on hotel accommodations. It costs $79 per night to stay at the Sunset Beach Lodge. Is it within Nicole's budget to stay at the lodge for 6 nights?

   B. If Nicole plans to spend $\frac{1}{2}$ of the money on hotel accommodations and $\frac{1}{4}$ of it on food, about how much money will she have left to spend on souvenirs and entertainment?

4. Lucky Louise went bargain hunting. She found a fan for $0.65, 7 matching pens for $0.15 apiece, and a special on pencils—5 for $1.60. If she buys 2 fans, all 7 matching pens, and only 3 pencils, how much money will she spend?

5. As Brett and Reggie board the plane to return home, the temperature on Faraway Island is 90°F. Brett must return to Minneapolis where it is -10°F. Reggie must return to Milwaukee where it is -7°F.

   A. Where is it colder, Minneapolis or Milwaukee? How much colder?

   B. What is the difference in temperature between Minneapolis and Faraway Island?

164 DAB • Grade 5 • Unit 10   MAPS AND COORDINATES

Discovery Assignment Book - page 164

*Answers for all the Home Practice in the *Discovery Assignment Book* are at the end of the unit.

Use the map to answer the following questions. The origin of the map is at the corner of State Street and Madison Street. Measure distances from the entrance to each location. The entrance is marked with an Ⓔ. Measure all walking distances along streets.

1. If you walk from the Sears Tower to Buckingham Fountain, about how far would you walk?

2. If you walk from (-6, -3) to (-1, -3) to (0, 0), about how far would you walk?

3. If you park in the Grant Park Garage and then go to the Opera House, about how far would you walk?

4. If you were at (1, -7), about how far would you walk to get to the Merchandise Mart?

Assessment Blackline Master

Unit Resource Guide - page 122

Unit Resource Guide (p. 122)

Carol's Chicago Map

1. about $1\frac{6}{8}$ miles or $1\frac{3}{4}$ miles

2. about $1\frac{1}{8}$ miles

3. a little more than 1 mile

4. about $2\frac{4}{8}$ or $2\frac{1}{2}$ miles

Optional Lesson 9

Escher Drawings

Estimated Class Sessions

1

Lesson Overview

Students are introduced to the works of M.C. Escher. Students use a tessellating figure to create Escher-like art. This activity can be an excellent art lesson.

Key Content

- Using tessellations to create art.
- Connecting mathematics and art.

Key Vocabulary

- tessellation

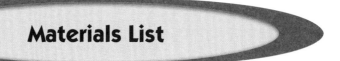

Curriculum Sequence

Before This Unit

In Unit 6 Lesson 5, students were introduced to tessellations in quilts.

Materials List

Supplies and Copies

Student	Teacher
Supplies for Each Student • several index cards • 1 piece of newsprint or other large paper preferably greater than 8″ × 10″ plus extras • scissors • tape	**Supplies**
Copies	**Copies/Transparencies** • 1 transparency of *Creating Escher-like Drawings,* optional (*Unit Resource Guide* Page 132)

All blackline masters including assessment, transparency, and DPP masters are also on the Teacher Resource CD.

Student Books

Escher Drawings (*Student Guide* Page 345)

Before the Activity

You may wish to find a book on M.C. Escher that has reproductions of some of his works.

Teaching the Activity

Ask students to open to the *Escher Drawings* Activity Page in the *Student Guide.* Give students a chance to read the opening paragraph about M.C. Escher (Maurits Cornelis Escher) and look at the first drawing, *Symmetry Drawing with Pegasus.* Explain that Pegasus is the name of the winged horse in Greek mythology.

In *Question 1,* students should see that there are two colors of winged horses, brown and white. It is interesting to note how alternating colors make the creatures appear to be flying. Except for color, the horses are identical. Children might note they are all facing the same direction. If students studied tessellations in Unit 6, ask them whether this is a tessellation. Since this shape forms a pattern without gaps or overlaps, it is a tessellation. If the concept was not covered earlier, introduce the idea of a **tessellation.**

In *Question 2,* students might describe the slides as horizontal or on a diagonal. We can say that the tessellation is formed by doing many slides.

The next drawing shows another example of Escher's art called *Symmetry Drawing with Fish.* In this picture, a slide is not enough to move a pink fish onto a red fish. Actually, a rotation (turn) is needed. In *Question 3* students should notice that adjacent rows of fish are swimming in opposite directions. This contrasts to the previous picture where the horses were all facing the same direction *(Question 4).*

As fantastic as it may seem, Escher used a square to create *Symmetry Drawing with Pegasus,* and began with a quadrilateral to create *Symmetry Drawing with Fish.*

Making Escher-like drawings is not difficult. To begin, show students an example. Follow the example provided or make your own.

Refer to the *Creating Escher-like Drawings* Transparency Master in the *Unit Resource Guide.* In this example, we begin with a rectangle, a shape we know tessellates. Use an index card to demonstrate the steps to students. To create a design that tessellates, cut a piece from one side of the index card and tape the cut-out piece to the opposite side,

Escher Drawings

M.C. Escher was a Dutch artist who used many mathematical ideas to create his works. Escher was born in 1898 and died in 1972. Escher often began with a tessellating shape, such as a square or a hexagon. He changed these shapes so that they looked like other objects, such as animals. The changes were made so that the final shape also tessellated. Escher then used slides and turns, along with interesting details on the shapes, to create his art.

Discuss

This picture at the right is called *Symmetry Drawing with Pegasus.*

1. Describe the horses you see in the picture.

2. Describe the slides you see in the picture.

Below is another Escher drawing called *Symmetry Drawing with Fish.*

M.C. Escher's Symmetry Drawings © 1996 Cordon Art-Baarn-Holland.

3. Describe the fish you see in the picture.

4. Describe the slides you see in the picture.

5. Look at the direction the pink fish are swimming and the direction the red fish are swimming. Do you see a difference?

6. Compare the two pictures. What is the same about them? What is different about them?

M.C. Escher's Symmetry Drawings © 1996 Cordon Art-Baarn-Holland.

Escher Drawings   SG • Grade 5 • Unit 10 • Lesson 9   **345**

Student Guide - page 345 *(Answers on p. 133)*

Content Note

Tessellating Shapes. All triangles and all quadrilaterals tessellate. Thus, any triangle or any quadrilateral could be used to begin an Escher-like drawing.

as shown on the top of the Transparency Master (steps 2 and 3). You may repeat this if you like (steps 4 and 5). Then decorate the shape to make an interesting figure.

Seeing *Creating Escher-like Drawings* on the overhead will help students see how the figure is formed.

To show students how the figure you created might be tessellated, trace the shape several times on a blank overhead or the board. The bottom of the *Creating Escher-like Drawings* shows how you might do this.

Each child can now cut an index card (give each child several) to construct his or her own figure. The student can use the figure to create a picture on a large piece of newsprint or similar medium.

Estimated Class Sessions

1

At a Glance

Teaching the Activity

1. Introduce students to the work of M.C. Escher by reading together the introduction on the *Escher Drawings* Activity Page in the *Student Guide.*

2. Discuss the two Escher drawings that appear in the *Student Guide.*

3. Show students how to make a figure that will tessellate and form an Escher-like drawing from an index card. Use the *Creating Escher-like Drawings* Transparency Master to assist you.

4. Trace the figure you created on the overhead or board to show students how to form a tessellation.

5. Students use an index card, scissors, and tape to create their own figures. They then use the figures to create pictures on newsprint.

Answer Key is on page 133.

Notes:

Creating Escher-like Drawings

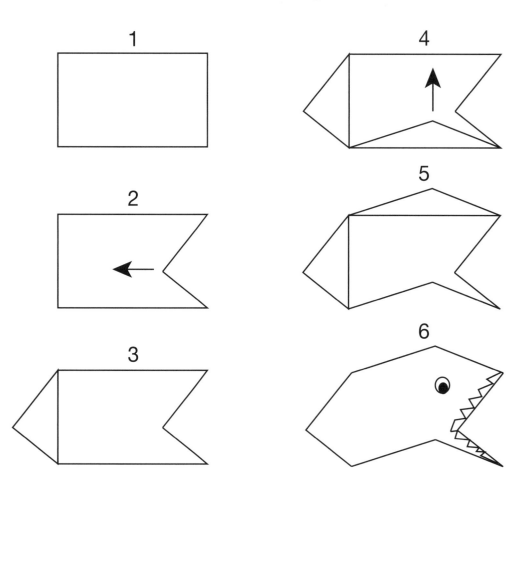

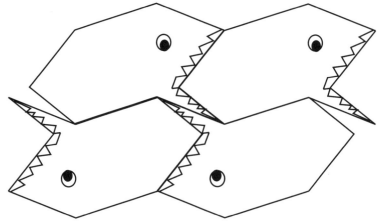

Transparency Master

Student Guide (p. 345)

Escher Drawings

1. Answers will vary. There are two colors of winged horses, brown and white. The shapes of the horses are identical. They are all facing the same direction. It is an example of a tessellation.*

2. Answers will vary. There are many slides. The slide may be described as horizontal or on a diagonal.*

3. Answers will vary. There are pink and red fish. The shapes of the fish are identical. Adjacent rows of fish are swimming in opposite directions.*

4. Slides will move pink fish to pink fish and red fish to red fish. However, you can not slide a pink fish onto a red fish.*

5. Adjacent rows of fish are swimming in opposite directions.

6. The horses all face the same direction whereas adjacent rows of fish are swimming in opposite directions. Slides can be used to move a horse onto every other horse. This is not true for the fish.

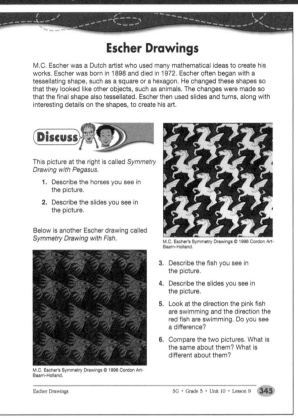

Student Guide - page 345

---

*Answers and/or discussion are included in the Lesson Guide.

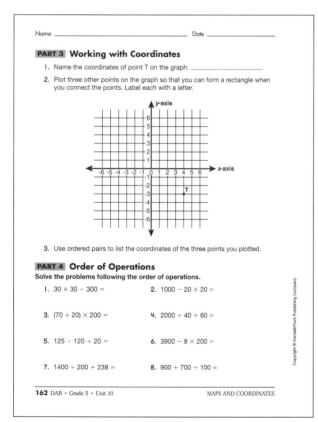

Discovery Assignment Book - page 161

Discovery Assignment Book (p. 161)

Part 1. Division Practice

A. 147 R1

B. 1356

C. 19 R61

D. 600

Part 2. Negative Numbers

1. 10, 8, 6, 4, 2, 0, -2, -4, -6, -8, -10

2. 12, 9, 6, 3, 0, -3, -6, -9, -12

3. -20, -16, -12, -8, -4, 0, 4, 8, 12, 16, 20

4. -8°F

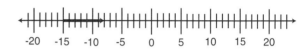

Discovery Assignment Book (p. 162)

Part 3. Working with Coordinates

1. (4, -3)

2. Answers will vary. A sample rectangle is shown below.

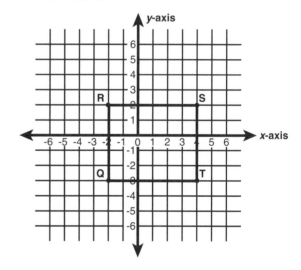

3. Answers will vary. The coordinates of the vertices of the sample rectangle shown in Question 2 are: Q is at (-2, -3), R is at (-2, 2), and S is at (4, 2).

Part 4. Order of Operations

1. 600

2. 600

3. 18,000

4. 110

5. 119

6. 2300

7. 245

8. 907

Discovery Assignment Book - page 162

Discovery Assignment Book (p. 163)

Part 5. Practicing the Operations

I. **A.** 156.40   **B.** 23,490

   C. 8330   **D.** $34.54

   E. 174 R10   **F.** 379

   G. 0.288   **H.** 79 R2

   I. 8247

2. **A.** Answers will vary.

   Possible response: $2 \times 70 = 140$

   B. Answers will vary: $260 \times 100 = 26,000$

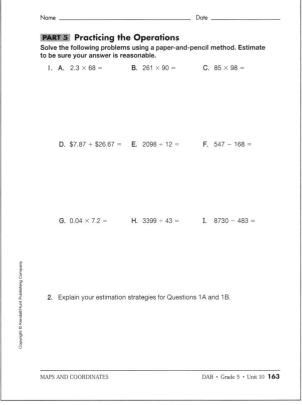

Name _____ Date _____

PART 5 Practicing the Operations
Solve the following problems using a paper-and-pencil method. Estimate to be sure your answer is reasonable.

I. **A.** $2.3 \times 68 =$ **B.** $261 \times 90 =$ **C.** $85 \times 98 =$

   D. $\$7.87 + \$26.67 =$ **E.** $2098 \div 12 =$ **F.** $547 - 168 =$

   G. $0.04 \times 7.2 =$ **H.** $3399 \div 43 =$ **I.** $8730 - 483 =$

2. Explain your estimation strategies for Questions 1A and 1B.

MAPS AND COORDINATES   DAB • Grade 5 • Unit 10 **163**

Discovery Assignment Book - page 163

Discovery Assignment Book (p. 164)

Part 6. Sunny Vacation

I. Get-Up-And-Go Travel Agency; 452.99×2 is more than $900.

2. Estimates will vary. She will have $1547.01 to spend; $1547.01 \div 7$ is about $200 a day.

3. **A.** Yes. She wants to spend $500 on hotel accommodations; 79×5 is about $400.

   B. $250

4. $3.31

5. **A.** Minneapolis; 3 degrees colder

   B. 100 degrees

Name _____ Date _____

PART 6 Sunny Vacation
Choose an appropriate method to solve each of the following problems. For some questions you may need to find an exact answer, while for others you may only need an estimate. For each question, you may choose to use paper and pencil, mental math, or a calculator. Use a separate sheet of paper to explain how you solved each problem.

I. Brett and Reggie plan to fly away to Faraway Island. The Get-Up-And-Go Travel Agency has a sale in progress. If you buy one round trip ticket for $899.99, you will get a second ticket free. Global Travel is offering round trip tickets to Faraway Island for $452.99. Which travel agency offers the best deal for Brett and Reggie? Why?

2. Joanne is going to Faraway Island by herself for seven days. She has $2000 to spend. If she buys one airline ticket from Global Travel, about how much money can she spend each day?

3. Nicole won a free airline ticket to Faraway Island. She has $1000 to spend while she is there.
   A. Nicole plans to spend $\frac{1}{2}$ of the money on hotel accommodations. It costs $79 per night to stay at the Sunset Beach Lodge. Is it within Nicole's budget to stay at the lodge for 6 nights?
   B. If Nicole plans to spend $\frac{1}{2}$ of the money on hotel accommodations and $\frac{1}{4}$ of it on food, about how much money will she have left to spend on souvenirs and entertainment?

4. Lucky Louise went bargain hunting. She found a fan for $0.65, 7 matching pens for $0.15 apiece, and a special on pencils—5 for $1.60. If she buys 2 fans, all 7 matching pens, and only 3 pencils, how much money will she spend?

5. As Brett and Reggie board the plane to return home, the temperature on Faraway Island is 90°F. Brett must return to Minneapolis where it is -10°F. Reggie must return to Milwaukee where it is -7°F.
   A. Where is it colder, Minneapolis or Milwaukee? How much colder?
   B. What is the difference in temperature between Minneapolis and Faraway Island?

164 DAB • Grade 5 • Unit 10   MAPS AND COORDINATES

Discovery Assignment Book - page 164

Glossary

This glossary provides definitions of key vocabulary terms in the Grade 5 lessons. Locations of key vocabulary terms in the curriculum are included with each definition. Components Key: URG = *Unit Resource Guide* and SG = *Student Guide*.

A

Acute Angle (URG Unit 6; SG Unit 6)
An angle that measures less than 90°.

Acute Triangle (URG Unit 6 & Unit 15; SG Unit 6 & Unit 15)
A triangle that has only acute angles.

All-Partials Multiplication Method (URG Unit 2)
A paper-and-pencil method for solving multiplication problems. Each partial product is recorded on a separate line. (*See also* partial product.)

$$\begin{array}{r} 186 \\ \times\ 3 \\ \hline 18 \\ 240 \\ 300 \\ \hline 558 \end{array}$$

Altitude of a Triangle (URG Unit 15; SG Unit 15)
A line segment from a vertex of a triangle perpendicular to the opposite side or to the line extending the opposite side; also, the length of this line. The altitude is also called the height of the triangle.

Angle (URG Unit 6; SG Unit 6)
The amount of turning or the amount of opening between two rays that have the same endpoint.

Arc (URG Unit 14; SG Unit 14)
Part of a circle between two points. (*See also* circle.)

Area (URG Unit 4 & Unit 15; SG Unit 4 & Unit 15)
A measurement of size. The area of a shape is the amount of space it covers, measured in square units.

Average (URG Unit 1 & Unit 4; SG Unit 1 & Unit 4)
A number that can be used to represent a typical value in a set of data. (*See also* mean, median, and mode.)

Axes (URG Unit 10; SG Unit 10)
Reference lines on a graph. In the Cartesian coordinate system, the axes are two perpendicular lines that meet at the origin. The singular of axes is axis.

B

Base of a Triangle (URG Unit 15; SG Unit 15)
One of the sides of a triangle; also, the length of the side. A perpendicular line drawn from the vertex opposite the base is called the height or altitude of the triangle.

Base of an Exponent (URG Unit 2; SG Unit 2)
When exponents are used, the number being multiplied. In $3^4 = 3 \times 3 \times 3 \times 3 = 81$, the 3 is the base and the 4 is the exponent. The 3 is multiplied by itself 4 times.

Base-Ten Pieces (URG Unit 2; SG Unit 2)
A set of manipulatives used to model our number system as shown in the figure below. Note that a skinny is made of 10 bits, a flat is made of 100 bits, and a pack is made of 1000 bits.

Base-Ten Shorthand (URG Unit 2)
A graphical representation of the base-ten pieces as shown below.

Nickname	Picture	Shorthand
bit	▱	·
skinny	▭	/
flat	▱	▱
pack	▱	▱

Benchmarks (SG Unit 7)
Numbers convenient for comparing and ordering numbers, e.g., $0, \frac{1}{2}, 1$ are convenient benchmarks for comparing and ordering fractions.

Best-Fit Line (URG Unit 3; SG Unit 3)
The line that comes closest to the points on a point graph.

Binning Data (URG Unit 8; SG Unit 8)
Placing data from a data set with a large number of values or large range into intervals in order to more easily see patterns in the data.

Bit (URG Unit 2; SG Unit 2)
A cube that measures 1 cm on each edge.
It is the smallest of the base-ten pieces and is often used to represent 1. (*See also* base-ten pieces.)

C

Cartesian Coordinate System (URG Unit 10; SG Unit 10)
A method of locating points on a flat surface by means of an ordered pair of numbers. This method is named after its originator, René Descartes. (*See also* coordinates.)

Categorical Variable (URG Unit 1; SG Unit 1)
Variables with values that are not numbers. (*See also* variable and value.)

Center of a Circle (URG Unit 14; SG Unit 14)
The point such that every point on a circle is the same distance from it. (*See also* circle.)

Centiwheel (URG Unit 7; SG Unit 7)
A circle divided into 100 equal sections used in exploring fractions, decimals, and percents.

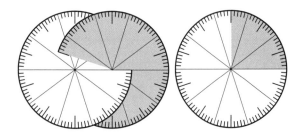

Central Angle (URG Unit 14; SG Unit 14)
An angle whose vertex is at the center of a circle.

Certain Event (URG Unit 7; SG Unit 7)
An event that has a probability of 1 (100%).

Chord (URG Unit 14; SG Unit 14)
A line segment that connects two points on a circle. (*See also* circle.)

Circle (URG Unit 14; SG Unit 14)
A curve that is made up of all the points that are the same distance from one point, the center.

Circumference (URG Unit 14; SG Unit 14)
The distance around a circle.

Common Denominator (URG Unit 5 & Unit 11; SG Unit 5 & Unit 11)
A denominator that is shared by two or more fractions. A common denominator is a common multiple of the denominators of the fractions. 15 is a common denominator of $\frac{2}{3} (= \frac{10}{15})$ and $\frac{4}{5} (= \frac{12}{15})$ since 15 is divisible by both 3 and 5.

Common Fraction (URG Unit 7; SG Unit 7)
Any fraction that is written with a numerator and denominator that are whole numbers. For example, $\frac{3}{4}$ and $\frac{9}{4}$ are both common fractions. (*See also* decimal fraction.)

Commutative Property of Addition (URG Unit 2)
The order of the addends in an addition problem does not matter, e.g., $7 + 3 = 3 + 7$.

Commutative Property of Multiplication (URG Unit 2)
The order of the factors in a multiplication problem does not matter, e.g., $7 \times 3 = 3 \times 7$. (*See also* turn-around facts.)

Compact Method (URG Unit 2)
Another name for what is considered the traditional multiplication algorithm.

$$\begin{array}{r} {}^{2}{}^{1}186 \\ \times\ 3 \\ \hline 558 \end{array}$$

Composite Number (URG Unit 11; SG Unit 11)
A number that has more than two distinct factors. For example, 9 has three factors (1, 3, 9) so it is a composite number.

Concentric Circles (URG Unit 14; SG Unit 14)
Circles that have the same center.

Congruent (URG Unit 6 & Unit 10; SG Unit 6)
Figures that are the same shape and size. Polygons are congruent when corresponding sides have the same length and corresponding angles have the same measure.

Conjecture (URG Unit 11; SG Unit 11)
A statement that has not been proved to be true, nor shown to be false.

Convenient Number (URG Unit 2; SG Unit 2)
A number used in computation that is close enough to give a good estimate, but is also easy to compute with mentally, e.g., 25 and 30 are convenient numbers for 27.

Convex (URG Unit 6)
A shape is convex if for any two points in the shape, the line segment between the points is also inside the shape.

Coordinates (URG Unit 10; SG Unit 10)
An ordered pair of numbers that locates points on a flat surface relative to a pair of coordinate axes. For example, in the ordered pair (4, 5), the first number (coordinate) is the distance from the point to the vertical axis and the second coordinate is the distance from the point to the horizontal axis. (*See also* axes.)

Corresponding Parts (URG Unit 10; SG Unit 10)
Matching parts in two or more figures. In the figure below, Sides AB and A′B′ are corresponding parts.

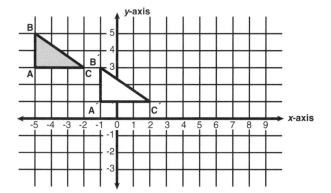

Cryptography (SG Unit 11) The study of secret codes.

Cubic Centimeter (URG Unit 13)
The volume of a cube that is one centimeter long on each edge.

D

Data (SG Unit 1)
Information collected in an experiment or survey.

Decagon (URG Unit 6; SG Unit 6)
A ten-sided, ten-angled polygon.

Decimal (URG Unit 7; SG Unit 7)
1. A number written using the base ten place value system.
2. A number containing a decimal point.

Decimal Fraction (URG Unit 7; SG Unit 7)
A fraction written as a decimal. For example, 0.75 and 0.4 are decimal fractions and $\frac{75}{100}$ and $\frac{4}{10}$ are the equivalent common fractions.

Degree (URG Unit 6; SG Unit 6)
A degree (°) is a unit of measure for angles. There are 360 degrees in a circle.

Denominator (URG Unit 3; SG Unit 3)
The number below the line in a fraction. The denominator indicates the number of equal parts in which the unit whole is divided. For example, the 5 is the denominator in the fraction $\frac{2}{5}$. In this case the unit whole is divided into five equal parts. (*See also* numerator.)

Density (URG Unit 13; SG Unit 13)
The ratio of an object's mass to its volume.

Diagonal (URG Unit 6)
A line segment that connects nonadjacent corners of a polygon.

Diameter (URG Unit 14; SG Unit 14)
1. A line segment that connects two points on a circle and passes through the center.
2. The length of this line segment.

Digit (SG Unit 2)
Any one of the ten symbols 0, 1, 2, 3, 4, 5, 6, 7, 8, 9. The number 37 is made up of the digits 3 and 7.

Dividend (URG Unit 4 & Unit 9; SG Unit 4 & Unit 9)
The number that is divided in a division problem, e.g., 12 is the dividend in 12 ÷ 3 = 4.

Divisor (URG Unit 2, Unit 4, & Unit 9; SG Unit 2, Unit 4, & Unit 9)
In a division problem, the number by which another number is divided. In the problem 12 ÷ 4 = 3, the 4 is the divisor, the 12 is the dividend, and the 3 is the quotient.

Dodecagon (URG Unit 6; SG Unit 6)
A twelve-sided, twelve-angled polygon.

E

Endpoint (URG Unit 6; SG Unit 6)
The point at either end of a line segment or the point at the end of a ray.

Equally Likely (URG Unit 7; SG Unit 7)
When events have the same probability, they are called equally likely.

Equidistant (URG Unit 14)
At the same distance.

Equilateral Triangle (URG Unit 6, Unit 14, & Unit 15)
A triangle that has all three sides equal in length. An equilateral triangle also has three equal angles.

Equivalent Fractions (URG Unit 3; SG Unit 3)
Fractions that have the same value, e.g., $\frac{2}{4} = \frac{1}{2}$.

Estimate (URG Unit 2; SG Unit 2)
1. To find *about* how many (as a verb).
2. A number that is *close to* the desired number (as a noun).

Expanded Form (SG Unit 2)
A way to write numbers that shows the place value of each digit, e.g., 4357 = 4000 + 300 + 50 + 7.

Exponent (URG Unit 2 & Unit 11; SG Unit 2 & Unit 11)
The number of times the base is multiplied by itself. In $3^4 = 3 \times 3 \times 3 \times 3 = 81$, the 3 is the base and the 4 is the exponent. The 3 is multiplied by itself 4 times.

Extrapolation (URG Unit 13; SG Unit 13)
Using patterns in data to make predictions or to estimate values that lie beyond the range of values in the set of data.

F

Fact Families (URG Unit 2; SG Unit 2)
Related math facts, e.g., 3 × 4 = 12, 4 × 3 = 12, 12 ÷ 3 = 4, 12 ÷ 4 = 3.

Factor Tree (URG Unit 11; SG Unit 11)
A diagram that shows the prime factorization of a number.

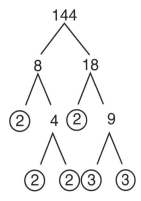

Factors (URG Unit 2 & Unit 11; SG Unit 2 & Unit 11)
1. In a multiplication problem, the numbers that are multiplied together. In the problem $3 \times 4 = 12$, 3 and 4 are the factors.
2. Numbers that divide a number evenly, e.g., 1, 2, 3, 4, 6, and 12 are all the factors of 12.

Fair Game (URG Unit 7; SG Unit 7)
A game in which it is equally likely that any player will win.

Fewest Pieces Rule (URG Unit 2)
Using the least number of base-ten pieces to represent a number. (*See also* base-ten pieces.)

Fixed Variables (URG Unit 4; SG Unit 3 & Unit 4)
Variables in an experiment that are held constant or not changed, in order to find the relationship between the manipulated and responding variables. These variables are often called controlled variables. (*See also* manipulated variable and responding variable.)

Flat (URG Unit 2; SG Unit 2)
A block that measures 1 cm $\times$ 10 cm $\times$ 10 cm. It is one of the base-ten pieces and is often used to represent 100. (*See also* base-ten pieces.)

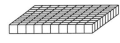

Flip (URG Unit 10; SG Unit 10)
A motion of the plane in which the plane is reflected over a line so that any point and its image are the same distance from the line.

Forgiving Division Method
(URG Unit 4; SG Unit 4)
A paper-and-pencil method for division in which successive partial quotients are chosen and subtracted from the dividend, until the remainder is less than the divisor. The sum of the partial quotients is the quotient. For example, $644 \div 7$ can be solved as shown at the right.

```
            92
    7 ) 644
        140  | 20
        504
        350  | 50
        154
        140  | 20
         14
         14  |  2
          0  | 92
```

Formula (SG Unit 11 & Unit 14)
A number sentence that gives a general rule. A formula for finding the area of a rectangle is Area = length $\times$ width, or $A = l \times w$.

Fraction (URG Unit 7; SG Unit 7)
A number that can be written as a/b where a and b are whole numbers and b is not zero.

G

Googol (URG Unit 2)
A number that is written as a 1 with 100 zeroes after it (10^{100}).

Googolplex (URG Unit 2)
A number that is written as a 1 with a googol of zeroes after it.

H

Height of a Triangle (URG Unit 15; SG Unit 15)
A line segment from a vertex of a triangle perpendicular to the opposite side or to the line extending the opposite side; also, the length of this line. The height is also called the altitude.

Hexagon (URG Unit 6; SG Unit 6)
A six-sided polygon.

Hypotenuse (URG Unit 15; SG Unit 15)
The longest side of a right triangle.

I

Image (URG Unit 10; SG Unit 10)
The result of a transformation, in particular a slide (translation) or a flip (reflection), in a coordinate plane. The new figure after the slide or flip is the image of the old figure.

Impossible Event (URG Unit 7; SG Unit 7)
An event that has a probability of 0 or 0%.

Improper Fraction (URG Unit 3; SG Unit 3)
A fraction in which the numerator is greater than or equal to the denominator. An improper fraction is greater than or equal to one.

Infinite (URG Unit 2)
Never ending, immeasurably great, unlimited.

Interpolation (URG Unit 13; SG Unit 13)
Making predictions or estimating values that lie between data points in a set of data.

Intersect (URG Unit 14)
To meet or cross.

Isosceles Triangle (URG Unit 6 & Unit 15)
A triangle that has at least two sides of equal length.

J

K

L

Lattice Multiplication
(URG Unit 9; SG Unit 9)
A method for multiplying that
uses a lattice to arrange the
partial products so the digits are
correctly placed in the correct
place value columns. A lattice
for $43 \times 96 = 4128$ is shown at
the right.

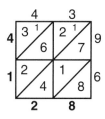

Legs of a Right Triangle (URG Unit 15; SG Unit 15)
The two sides of a right triangle that form the right angle.

Length of a Rectangle (URG Unit 4 & Unit 15;
SG Unit 4 & Unit 15)
The distance along one side of a rectangle.

Line
A set of points that form a straight path extending infinitely in two directions.

Line of Reflection (URG Unit 10)
A line that acts as a mirror so that after a shape is flipped over the line, corresponding points are at the same distance (equidistant) from the line.

Line Segment (URG Unit 14)
A part of a line between and including two points, called the endpoints.

Liter (URG Unit 13)
Metric unit used to measure volume. A liter is a little more than a quart.

Lowest Terms (SG Unit 11)
A fraction is in lowest terms if the numerator and denominator have no common factor greater than 1.

M

Manipulated Variable (URG Unit 4; SG Unit 4)
In an experiment, the variable with values known at the beginning of the experiment. The experimenter often chooses these values before data is collected. The manipulated variable is often called the independent variable.

Mass (URG Unit 13)
The amount of matter in an object.

Mean (URG Unit 1 & Unit 4; SG Unit 1 & Unit 4)
An average of a set of numbers that is found by adding the values of the data and dividing by the number of values.

Measurement Division (URG Unit 4)
Division as equal grouping. The total number of objects and the number of objects in each group are known. The number of groups is the unknown. For example, tulip bulbs come in packages of 8. If 216 bulbs are sold, how many packages are sold?

Median (URG Unit 1; SG Unit 1)
For a set with an odd number of data arranged in order, it is the middle number. For an even number of data arranged in order, it is the mean of the two middle numbers.

Meniscus (URG Unit 13)
The curved surface formed when a liquid creeps up the side of a container (for example, a graduated cylinder).

Milliliter (ml) (URG Unit 13)
A measure of capacity in the metric system that is the volume of a cube that is one centimeter long on each side.

Mixed Number (URG Unit 3; SG Unit 3)
A number that is written as a whole number followed by a fraction. It is equal to the sum of the whole number and the fraction.

Mode (URG Unit 1; SG Unit 1)
The most common value in a data set.

Mr. Origin (URG Unit 10; SG Unit 10)
A plastic figure used to represent the origin of a coordinate system and to indicate the directions of the x- and y- axes. (and possibly the z-axis).

N

N-gon (URG Unit 6; SG Unit 6)
A polygon with N sides.

Negative Number (URG Unit 10; SG Unit 10)
A number less than zero; a number to the left of zero on a horizontal number line.

Nonagon (URG Unit 6; SG Unit 6)
A nine-sided polygon.

Numerator (URG Unit 3; SG Unit 3)
The number written above the line in a fraction. For example, the 2 is the numerator in the fraction $\frac{2}{5}$. In this case, we are interested in two of the five parts. (*See also* denominator.)

Numerical Expression (URG Unit 4; SG Unit 4)
A combination of numbers and operations, e.g.,
$5 + 8 \div 4$.

Numerical Variable (URG Unit 1; SG Unit 1)
Variables with values that are numbers. (*See also* variable and value.)

O

Obtuse Angle (URG Unit 6; SG Unit 6)
An angle that measures more than 90°.

Obtuse Triangle (URG Unit 6 & Unit 15; SG Unit 6 & Unit 15)
A triangle that has an obtuse angle.

Octagon (URG Unit 6; SG Unit 6)
An eight-sided polygon.

Ordered Pair (URG Unit 10; SG Unit 10)
A pair of numbers that gives the coordinates of a point on a grid in relation to the origin. The horizontal coordinate is given first; the vertical coordinate is given second. For example, the ordered pair (5, 3) gives the coordinates of the point that is 5 units to the right of the origin and 3 units up.

Origin (URG Unit 10; SG Unit 10)
The point at which the x- and y-axes intersect on a coordinate plane. The origin is described by the ordered pair (0, 0) and serves as a reference point so that all the points on the plane can be located by ordered pairs.

P

Pack (URG Unit 2; SG Unit 2)
A cube that measures 10 cm on each edge. It is one of the base-ten pieces and is often used to represent 1000. (*See also* base-ten pieces.)

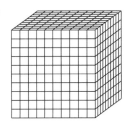

Parallel Lines (URG Unit 6 & Unit 10)
Lines that are in the same direction. In the plane, parallel lines are lines that do not intersect.

Parallelogram (URG Unit 6)
A quadrilateral with two pairs of parallel sides.

Partial Product (URG Unit 2)
One portion of the multiplication process in the all-partials multiplication method, e.g., in the problem 3×186 there are three partial products: $3 \times 6 = \underline{18}$, $3 \times 80 = \underline{240}$, and $3 \times 100 = \underline{300}$. (*See also* all-partials multiplication method.)

Partitive Division (URG Unit 4)
Division as equal sharing. The total number of objects and the number of groups are known. The number of objects in each group is the unknown. For example, Frank has 144 marbles that he divides equally into 6 groups. How many marbles are in each group?

Pentagon (URG Unit 6; SG Unit 6)
A five-sided polygon.

Percent (URG Unit 7; SG Unit 7)
Per hundred or out of 100. A special ratio that compares a number to 100. For example, 20% (twenty percent) of the jelly beans are yellow means that out of every 100 jelly beans, 20 are yellow.

Perimeter (URG Unit 15; SG Unit 15)
The distance around a two-dimensional shape.

Period (SG Unit 2)
A group of three places in a large number, starting on the right, often separated by commas as shown at the right.

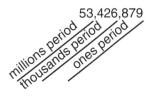

Perpendicular Lines (URG Unit 14 & Unit 15; SG Unit 14)
Lines that meet at right angles.

Pi (π) (URG Unit 14; SG Unit 14)
The ratio of the circumference to diameter of a circle. $\pi = 3.14159265358979. \ldots$ It is a nonterminating, nonrepeating decimal.

Place (SG Unit 2)
The position of a digit in a number.

Place Value (URG Unit 2; SG Unit 2)
The value of a digit in a number. For example, the 5 is in the hundreds place in 4573, so it stands for 500.

Polygon (URG Unit 6; SG Unit 6)
A two-dimensional connected figure made of line segments in which each endpoint of every side meets with an endpoint of exactly one other side.

Population (URG Unit 1 Unit 1)
A collection of persons or things whose properties will be analyzed in a survey or experiment.

Portfolio (URG Unit 2; SG Unit 2)
A collection of student work that show how a student's skills, attitudes, and knowledge change over time.

Positive Number (URG Unit 10; SG Unit 10)
A number greater than zero; a number to the right of zero on a horizontal number line.

Power (URG Unit 2; SG Unit 2)
An exponent. Read 10^4 as, "ten to the fourth power" or "ten to the fourth." We say 10,000 or 10^4 is the fourth power of ten.

Prime Factorization (URG Unit 11; SG Unit 11)
Writing a number as a product of primes. The prime factorization of 100 is $2 \times 2 \times 5 \times 5$.

Prime Number (URG Unit 11; SG Unit 11)
A number that has exactly two factors: itself and 1. For example, 7 has exactly two distinct factors, 1 and 7.

Probability (URG Unit 7; SG Unit 1 & Unit 7)
A number from 0 to 1 (0% to 100%) that describes how likely an event is to happen. The closer that the probability of an event is to one, the more likely the event will happen.

Product (URG Unit 2; SG Unit 2)
The answer to a multiplication problem. In the problem $3 \times 4 = 12$, 12 is the product.

Proper Fraction (URG Unit 3; SG Unit 3)
A fraction in which the numerator is less than the denominator. Proper fractions are less than one.

Proportion (URG Unit 3 & Unit 13; SG Unit 13)
A statement that two ratios are equal.

Protractor (URG Unit 6; SG Unit 6)
A tool for measuring angles.

Q

Quadrants (URG Unit 10; SG Unit 10)
The four sections of a coordinate grid that are separated by the axes.

Quadrilateral (URG Unit 6; SG Unit 6)
A polygon with four sides. (*See also* polygon.)

Quotient (URG Unit 4 & Unit 9; SG Unit 2, Unit 4, & Unit 9)
The answer to a division problem. In the problem $12 \div 3 = 4$, the 4 is the quotient.

R

Radius (URG Unit 14; SG Unit 14)
1. A line segment connecting the center of a circle to any point on the circle.
2. The length of this line segment.

Ratio (URG Unit 3 & Unit 12; SG Unit 3 & Unit 13)
A way to compare two numbers or quantities using division. It is often written as a fraction.

Ray (URG Unit 6; SG Unit 6)
A part of a line with one endpoint that extends indefinitely in one direction.

Rectangle (URG Unit 6; SG Unit 6)
A quadrilateral with four right angles.

Reflection (URG Unit 10)
(*See* flip.)

Regular Polygon (URG Unit 6; SG Unit 6; DAB Unit 6)
A polygon with all sides of equal length and all angles equal.

Remainder (URG Unit 4 & Unit 9; SG Unit 4 & Unit 9)
Something that remains or is left after a division problem. The portion of the dividend that is not evenly divisible by the divisor, e.g., $16 \div 5 = 3$ with 1 as a remainder.

Repeating Decimals (SG Unit 9)
A decimal fraction with one or more digits repeating without end.

Responding Variable (URG Unit 4; SG Unit 4)
The variable whose values result from the experiment. Experimenters find the values of the responding variable by doing the experiment. The responding variable is often called the dependent variable.

Rhombus (URG Unit 6; SG Unit 6)
A quadrilateral with four equal sides.

Right Angle (URG Unit 6; SG Unit 6)
An angle that measures 90°.

Right Triangle (URG Unit 6 & Unit 15; SG Unit 6 & Unit 15)
A triangle that contains a right angle.

Rubric (URG Unit 1)
A scoring guide that can be used to guide or assess student work.

S

Sample (URG Unit 1)
A part or subset of a population.

Scalene Triangle (URG Unit 15)
A triangle that has no sides that are equal in length.

Scientific Notation (URG Unit 2; SG Unit 2)
A way of writing numbers, particularly very large or very small numbers. A number in scientific notation has two factors. The first factor is a number greater than or equal to one and less than ten. The second factor is a power of 10 written with an exponent. For example, 93,000,000 written in scientific notation is 9.3×10^7.

Septagon (URG Unit 6; SG Unit 6)
A seven-sided polygon.

Side-Angle-Side (URG Unit 6 & Unit 14)
A geometric property stating that two triangles having two corresponding sides with the included angle equal are congruent.

Side-Side-Side (URG Unit 6)
A geometric property stating that two triangles having corresponding sides equal are congruent.

Sides of an Angle (URG Unit 6; SG Unit 6)
The sides of an angle are two rays with the same endpoint. (*See also* endpoint and ray.)

Sieve of Eratosthenes (SG Unit 11)
A method for separating prime numbers from nonprime numbers developed by Eratosthenes, an Egyptian librarian, in about 240 BCE.

Similar (URG Unit 6; SG Unit 6)
Similar shapes have the same shape but not necessarily the same size.

Skinny (URG Unit 2; SG Unit 2)
A block that measures 1 cm × 1 cm × 10 cm.
It is one of the base-ten pieces
and is often used to represent 10.
(*See also* base-ten pieces.)

Slide (URG Unit 10; SG Unit 10)
Moving a geometric figure in the plane by moving every point of the figure the same distance in the same direction. Also called translation.

Speed (URG Unit 3 & Unit 5; SG Unit 3 & Unit 5)
The ratio of distance moved to time taken, e.g., 3 miles/1 hour or 3 mph is a speed.

Square (URG Unit 6 & Unit 14; SG Unit 6)
A quadrilateral with four equal sides and four right angles.

Square Centimeter (URG Unit 4; SG Unit 4)
The area of a square that is 1 cm long on each side.

Square Number (URG Unit 11)
A number that is the product of a whole number multiplied by itself. For example, 25 is a square number since $5 \times 5 = 25$. A square number can be represented by a square array with the same number of rows as columns. A square array for 25 has 5 rows of 5 objects in each row or 25 total objects.

Standard Form (SG Unit 2)
The traditional way to write a number, e.g., standard form for three hundred fifty-seven is 357. (*See also* expanded form and word form.)

Standard Units (URG Unit 4)
Internationally or nationally agreed-upon units used in measuring variables, e.g., centimeters and inches are standard units used to measure length and square centimeters and square inches are used to measure area.

Straight Angle (URG Unit 6; SG Unit 6)
An angle that measures 180º.

T

Ten Percent (URG Unit 4; SG Unit 4)
10 out of every hundred or $\frac{1}{10}$.

Tessellation (URG Unit 6 & Unit 10; SG Unit 6)
A pattern made up of one or more repeated shapes that completely covers a surface without any gaps or overlaps.

Translation
(*See* slide.)

Trapezoid (URG Unit 6)
A quadrilateral with exactly one pair of parallel sides.

Triangle (URG Unit 6; SG Unit 6)
A polygon with three sides.

Triangulating (URG Unit 6; SG Unit 6)
Partitioning a polygon into two or more nonoverlapping triangles by drawing diagonals that do not intersect.

Turn-Around Facts (URG Unit 2)
Multiplication facts that have the same factors but in a different order, e.g., $3 \times 4 = 12$ and $4 \times 3 = 12$. (*See also* commutative property of multiplication.)

Twin Primes (URG Unit 11; SG Unit 11)
A pair of prime numbers whose difference is 2. For example, 3 and 5 are twin primes.

U

Unit Ratio (URG Unit 13; SG Unit 13)
A ratio with a denominator of one.

V

Value (URG Unit 1; SG Unit 1)
The possible outcomes of a variable. For example, red, green, and blue are possible values for the variable *color*. Two meters and 1.65 meters are possible values for the variable *length*.

Variable (URG Unit 1; SG Unit 1)
1. An attribute or quantity that changes or varies. (*See also* categorical variable and numerical variable.)
2. A symbol that can stand for a variable.

Variables in Proportion (URG Unit 13; SG Unit 13)
When the ratio of two variables in an experiment is always the same, the variables are in proportion.

Velocity (URG Unit 5; SG Unit 5)
Speed in a given direction. Speed is the ratio of the distance traveled to time taken.

Vertex (URG Unit 6; SG Unit 6)
A common point of two rays or line segments that form an angle.

Volume (URG Unit 13)
The measure of the amount of space occupied by an object.

W

Whole Number
Any of the numbers 0, 1, 2, 3, 4, 5, 6 and so on.

Width of a Rectangle (URG Unit 4 & Unit 15; SG Unit 4 & Unit 15)
The distance along one side of a rectangle is the length and the distance along an adjacent side is the width.

Word Form (SG Unit 2)
A number expressed in words, e.g., the word form for 123 is "one hundred twenty-three." (*See also* expanded form and standard form.)

X

Y

Z